OPCS Surveys of Psychiatric
Morbidity in Great Britain

Report 6

KU-607-529

Economic activity and social functioning of residents with psychiatric disorders

Howard Meltzer

Baljit Gill

Mark Petticrew

Kerstin Hinds

London: HMSO

© Crown copyright 1996

ISBN 0 11 691663 X

Notice

On 1 April 1996 the Office of Population Censuses and Surveys and the Central Statistical Office merged to form the Office for National Statistics. The logo of the new Office appears on the front cover of this report but the report series name - 'OPCS Surveys of Psychiatric Morbidity in Great Britain' - remains unchanged, to preserve the continuity of the 8-report series. Reference to OPCS inside the report are also unchanged since it was already in production at the time of the merger.

Published by HMSO and available from:

HMSO Publications Centre
(Mail, fax and telephone orders only)
PO Box 276, London SW8 5DT
Telephone orders 0171 873 9090
General enquiries 0171 873 0011
(queuing system in operation for both numbers)
Fax orders 0171 873 8200

HMSO Bookshops
49 High Holborn, London WC1V 6HB
(counter service only)
0171 873 0011 Fax 0171 831 1326
68–69 Bull Street, Birmingham B4 6AD
0121 236 9696   Fax 0121 236 9699
33 Wine Street, Bristol BS1 2BQ
0117 9264306 Fax 0117 9294515
9–21 Princess Street, Manchester M60 8AS
0161 834 7201 Fax 0161 833 0634
16 Arthur Street, Belfast BT1 4GD
01232 238451 Fax 01232 235401
71 Lothian Road, Edinburgh EH3 9AZ
0131 228 4181 Fax 0131 229 2734
The HMSO Oriel Bookshop
The Friary, Cardiff CF1 4AA
01222 395548 Fax 01222 384347

HMSO's Accredited Agents
(see Yellow Pages)

and through good booksellers

Authors' acknowledgements

We would like to thank everybody who contributed to the survey and the production of this report. Administrators, medical, nursing and support staff in the establishments we visited were of great assistance to the OPCS interviewers not only in organising contact with respondents but helping as proxy informants when subjects could not manage an interview.

We were supported by our specialist colleagues in OPCS who carried out the sampling, fieldwork, coding and editing stages.

The project was steered by a group comprising the following, to whom thanks are due for assistance and specialist advice at various stages of the survey:

Department of Health:
Dr Rachel Jenkins (chair)
Dr Elaine Gadd
Ms Val Roberts
Ms Antonia Roberts

Psychiatric epidemiologists:
Professor Paul Bebbington
Dr Terry Brugha
Professor Glyn Lewis
Dr Mike Farrell
Dr Jacquie de Alarcon

Office of Population Censuses and Surveys:
Ms Jil Matheson
Dr Howard Meltzer
Ms Baljit Gill
Dr Mark Petticrew
Ms Kerstin Hinds

Most importantly, we would like to thank all the participants in the survey for their co-operation.

Contents

List of tables

Notes

1 Tables showing percentages

The row or column percentages may add to 99% or 101% because of rounding.

The varying positions of the percentage signs and bases in the tables denote the presentation of different types of information. Where there is a percentage sign at the head of a column and the base at the foot, the whole distribution is presented and the individual percentages add to between 99% and 101%. Where there is no percentage sign in the table and a note above the figures, the figures refer to the proportion of people who had the attribute being discussed, and the complementary proportion, to add to 100%, is not shown in the table.

Standard errors are shown in brackets beside percentages in the tables.

The following conventions have been used within tables showing percentages:
-     no cases
- 0   values less than 0.5%

2 Small bases

Very small bases have been avoided wherever possible because of the relatively high sampling errors that attach to small numbers. Often where the numbers are not large enough to justify the use of all categories, classifications have been condensed. However, an item within a classification is occasionally shown separately, even though the base is small, because to combine it with another large category would detract from the value of the larger category. In general, percentage distributions are shown if the base is 30 or more. Where the base is slightly lower, actual numbers are shown in square brackets

3 Significant differences

In general, this Report gives a description of the data rather than looking at differences, as small bases make such comparisons difficult. The few comparisons which are shown in the Report either reach statistical significance or show very big differences albeit on small bases. Care should be taken in interpreting such findings.

Focus of the report and survey definitions

Focus of the report

This Report is the last of the three to look at data from the OPCS survey of psychiatric morbidity among residents of institutions[1]. It presents results about adults living in hospitals, residential care homes and other types of residential accommodation; institutions whose primary purpose is the long term care of people with mental health disorders. People with mental disorders who were temporary residents of institutions, such as those in acute, short-stay NHS hospital facilities were excluded from the survey. This is a descriptive report, however data from the survey are available for secondary analysis to further explore the relationships observed[2]. The report covers:

* economic activity of residents
* difficulties with activities of daily living
* social functioning
* use of alcohol, drugs and tobacco

In subsequent chapters each of these factors is considered for the three main categories of disorder separately, and where appropriate by type of institution.

This introductory section explains how institutions were classified for the survey, which residents were eligible, and how their psychiatric disorders were assessed. It then describes the measures used for analysis in subsequent chapters.

Coverage of institutions

Although a fairly detailed classification of types of institutions was made during data collection, five main types of institution have been used for analysis.

Full descriptions of what constituted different degrees of supervision for the purposes of this survey are shown below.

Ordinary housing or recognised lodging

Unsupervised in ordinary housing with a degree of protection, eg from eviction if in rent arrears.

Supervised in ordinary housing with regular domiciliary supervision of personal care, household maintenance, hygiene safety and rent payments.

Recognised lodging where the landlady has been selected for qualities of kindness and standard of care. Supervises personal care, hygiene, and rent payments.

Group homes

Unsupervised group home where a group of people live together in an ordinary house, with protected rent and occasional visits.

Supervised group home where a group of people live together in an ordinary house but have regular (up to daily) visits by housekeeper for household maintenance. No care staff live in.

Clustered group homes where a warden lives nearby and makes regular domiciliary checks. Some are built around a quadrangle with the entrance by the warden's flat.

Hostels

Supervised hostel where care staff live in and are on call at night. Provide regular domiciliary supervision.

Higher supervision hostel where care staff are in attendance all night.

Classification of institutions used in the OPCS survey

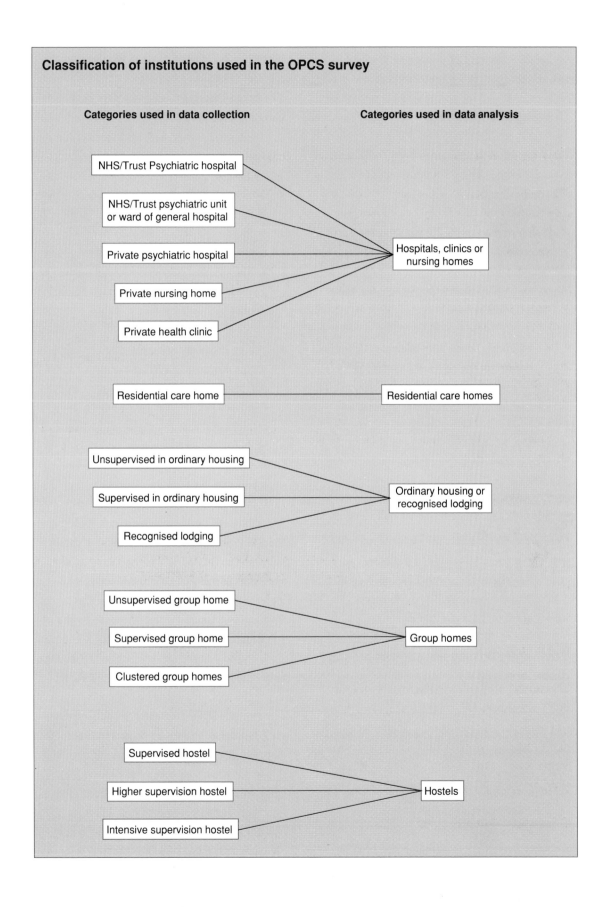

Categories used in data collection

Categories used in data analysis

- NHS/Trust Psychiatric hospital
- NHS/Trust psychiatric unit or ward of general hospital
- Private psychiatric hospital
- Private nursing home
- Private health clinic

→ Hospitals, clinics or nursing homes

- Residential care home → Residential care homes

- Unsupervised in ordinary housing
- Supervised in ordinary housing
- Recognised lodging

→ Ordinary housing or recognised lodging

- Unsupervised group home
- Supervised group home
- Clustered group homes

→ Group homes

- Supervised hostel
- Higher supervision hostel
- Intensive supervision hostel

→ Hostels

Intensive surpervision hostel with higher staff levels than above. For people with severe behaviour disturbance or disability.

Coverage of residents

Only **permanent residents** aged 16-64 were covered in the survey. A permanent resident was defined as:

* living in the sampled institution for the past six months;

* living in the sampled institution for less than 6 months but:

  • had been living in residential accommodation for the past six months, or

  • had no other permanent address, or

  • was likely to stay in the institution for the foreseeable future.

Proxy informants

Data were collected by proxy for some residents, and some topics could therefore not be covered in these circumstances. Individual chapters and Appendix B provide more information on proxy interviews.

Coverage and classification of mental disorders

In this report, we only consider residents who had one of the following three general categories of mental disorder:

• Schizophrenia, delusional or schizoaffective disorders

• Affective psychoses (mania and bipolar affective disorder)

• Neurotic disorders (Generalised Anxiety Disorder, depressive episode, mixed anxiety and depressive disorder, phobia, Obsessive-Compulsive Disorder, panic)

The approach used to assess psychotic psychopathology was to ask OPCS interviewers to find out from residents or staff information about clinical assessment and treatments by:

• asking residents directly what was the matter with them;

• asking staff, what was the matter with the subject, (if the subject could not answer but gave informed consent for another person to do so);

• asking residents or carers whether subjects were taking anti-psychotic drugs or having anti-psychotic injections;

• establishing whether residents had contact with any health care professional for a mental, nervous or emotional problem labelled as a psychotic illness.

The Clinical Interview Schedule (CIS-R) was used to identify neurotic disorders[3]. It establishes the existence of a particular neurotic symptom in the past month and leads the interviewer on to further enquiry giving a more detailed assessment of the symptom **in the past week**: frequency, duration, severity and time since onset. Algorithms are applied to the data to delineate six types of neurotic disorder.

The few residents identified (by self-report or staff-report) as having an organic mental disorder (2%), mental and behavioural disorders due to psychoactive substance abuse (1%), behavioural syndromes associated with psychological disturbances and physical factors (1%) or disorders of psychological development (1%) are excluded from consideration in this report.

Because of the absence of clinical research assessments for diagnostic classification, eg SCAN, care has to be taken in making comparisons of results presented in this report with those from the private household survey and other surveys among residents of institutions.

Measures and definitions used in this report

Economic activity

All adults were asked about their present working status and control of their financial affairs. Those who controlled their own finances, and who were not resident in hospitals, were then asked about receipt of social security benefits and sources of income in addition to social security benefits.

Activities of daily living

All adults, except those resident in hospitals, were asked about any difficulty they had with particular activities of daily living. The selection of activities was influenced by the topics covered in the MRC Needs for Care Assessment[4], and the OPCS Surveys of Disability[5]; the same questions were asked of adults in the OPCS private household survey of psychiatric morbidity[6]. The seven areas of functioning covered by the survey were:

- Personal care such as dressing, bathing, washing or using the toilet.

- Using transport to get out and about.

- Medical care such as taking medicines or pills, having injections or changes of dressing.

- Household activities such as preparing meals, shopping, laundry and housework.

- Practical activities such as gardening, decorating or doing household repairs.

- Dealing with paperwork, such as writing letters, sending cards or filling in forms.

- Managing money such as budgeting for food or paying bills.

Due to the domestic circumstances of residents of institutions, some of the above activities did not always apply. For example, a considerable proportion of adults in this survey were not involved in practical activities. Physical limitations as well as mental health problems could cause difficulties with many of the activities listed. Where there were sufficient cases in the sample, analyses were carried out separately for adults with and without a long standing physical complaint.

Adults with ADL difficulties were asked whether they required help for their difficulty, whether they received such help, and if so, who provided it.

Social functioning

This survey considered three aspects of social functioning; data were not collected on all aspects for all survey respondents:

a) Self-perceived social support was assessed for all adults with subject interviews; proxy data were not obtained

b) Social network size was obtained for all adults with a subject interview

c) information about involvement in social and leisure activities was obtained for all residents

a) Perceived social support

Perceived social support was assessed from respondents' answers to 7 questions taken from the 1987 Health and Lifestyle survey[7]. The seven questions take the form of statements which individuals could say were not true, partly true, or certainly true of their family and friends. Scores of 1 - 3 were obtained for each question and overall scores ranged from 7 to 21. The maximum score of 21 indicated no lack of social support, scores of 18 to 20 indicated a moderate lack of social support and scores of 17 and below showed that individuals perceived a severe lack of social support. The seven questions are listed below:

There are people I know - amongst my family or friends -

1) who do things to make me happy
2) who make me feel loved
3) who can be relied on no matter what happens
4) who would see that I am taken care of if I needed to be
5) who accept me just as I am
6) who make me feel an important part of their lives
7) who give me support and encouragement

Some adults in the survey reported having no close friends or relatives; these residents were classified as having a severe lack of social support. Where some of the 7 questions used to assess social support were not answered, the level of perceived social support was unclassified although it is possible that this group did in fact lack social support, and found the questions uncomfortable to answer.

b) **Extent of social networks**

In this survey information about social networks focused on the numbers of friends and relatives (aged 16 and over) respondents felt close to.

Data were collected about three groups of people:

1) adults who lived with respondents that respondents felt close to, including staff living on the premises
2) relatives who did not live with respondents that they felt close to
3) friends or acquaintances who did not live with respondents that would be described as close or good friends.

Close friends and relatives form an individual's 'primary support group'. Previous research has suggested that adults with a total primary support group of 3 people or fewer are at greatest risk of psychiatric morbidity[8][9].

c) **Leisure activities**

All residents were asked about the activities they did both in and out of the establishment during their leisure time. The lists of activities used in the survey were developed for the OPCS private household survey of psychiatric morbidity, drawing on previous work of a similar nature; 9 activities in the establishment and 15 outside the establishment were asked about. In this section, a measure of the total number of leisure time activities respondents participated in is first considered, followed by participation in specific activities in and out of the establishment. The number of activities are grouped as in the private household survey, as follows: 0-3, 4-9, 10 or more. In the general population, there was an association between participating in 3 or fewer leisure activities and having a psychiatric disorder.

Information is also presented about residents' attendance at four specific types of place for social activities, some catering specifically for those with mental health problems, and at Adult Education and Training centres.

Use of alcohol, drugs and tobacco

Measures of alcohol use, drug misuse, and cigarette smoking are available for residents who had personal interviews.

Drug misuse includes the use of illegal drugs such as cannabis, stimulants and hallucinogens, and the extra-medical use of prescription medicines. The consumption of prescribed medication in general was covered in Report 5 of this series of reports on psychiatric morbidity[10].

Obtaining information about people's drinking, drug-taking and cigarette smoking is difficult.

Social surveys of the general population consistently record lower levels of alcohol consumption and cigarette smoking than would be expected from alcohol and tobacco sales. This is for a variety of reasons, such as non-deliberate underestimation (for example of amounts drunk at home) and, particularly regarding drug misuse, due to respondents' concerns about confidentiality. More discussion of these problems is found in Report 3 of the private household survey[11]. However, it is not known whether, or to what extent, similar problems occur with regard to data collected in institutions.

Alcohol consumption

The methodology used on this survey to categorise alcohol consumption is the same as that used by the General Household Survey (GHS)[12] and the 1993 Health Survey for England[13].

All survey informants, with the exception of proxy informants, were asked how often they had drunk each of the following five types of drink in the previous year and how much of each type they usually drank on any one day:

- Shandy (excluding bottles or cans which have very low alcohol content)
- Beer, lager, stout, cider
- Spirits or liqueurs
- Sherry or martini
- Wine

To enable comparison between people who consumed different types of drink, informants described their consumption in terms of standard measures which contained similar amounts of alcohol, one unit of alcohol being approximately equivalent to a half pint of beer, a single measure of spirits (1/6 gill), a glass of wine (about 4.5 fluid ounces) or a small glass of sherry or fortified wine (2 fluid ounces).

The alcohol consumption rating is calculated by multiplying the number of units of each type of drink consumed on a 'usual' day by a conversion factor relating to the frequency with which it was drunk, and totalling across all drinks.

When the survey took place in 1994 the recommended sensible drinking levels were 21 units per week for men and 14 for women. At this time consumption above these levels was thought to be associated with increased health risks[14]. Although these levels were increased at the end of 1995, analysis of the data in this report is based on the 1994 guidelines to retain comparability with the data from the private household survey and the General Household Survey. Thus, residents who are described as being 'Fairly heavy' 'Heavy' or 'Very Heavy' drinkers were consuming over the recommended sensible level of alcohol when the survey took place. The way in which the descriptive labels used in the table relate to units of alcohol is shown below:

Alcohol consumption categories, based on usual weekly consumption (units) over the previous 12 months

Abstainer	Informant drank no alcohol in the past year	
Occasional drinker per week		Under 1 unit
	Men	Women
	(units per week)	
Light	1 - 10	1 - 7
Moderate	11 - 21	8 - 14
Over the recommended sensible level:		
Fairly heavy	22 - 35	15 - 25
Heavy	36 - 50	26 - 35
Very heavy	51 or more	36 or more

Alcohol dependence

In Report 3 of the private household survey of psychiatric morbidity three aspects of alcohol dependence were assessed: loss of control, symptomatic behaviour and binge drinking. For residents of institutions alcohol dependence was similarly measured.

Informants were classified as alcohol dependent if they responded positively to three or more of the following twelve statements:

Loss of control

1. Once I started drinking it was difficult for me to stop before I became completely drunk.

2. I sometimes kept on drinking after I had promised myself not to.

3. I deliberately tried to cut down or stop drinking, but I was unable to do so.

4. Sometimes I needed a drink so badly that I could not think of anything else.

Symptomatic behaviour

5. I have skipped a number of regular meals while drinking.

6. I have often had an alcoholic drink the first thing when I got up.

7. I have had a strong drink in the morning to get over the previous night's drinking.

8. I have woken up the next day not being able to remember some of the things I had done while drinking.

9. My hands shook a lot in the morning after drinking.

10. I need more alcohol than I used to, to get the same effect as before.

11. Sometimes I have woken up during the night or early morning sweating all over because of drinking.

12. I have stayed drunk for several days at a time.

Adults were defined as having 'loss of control' or 'symptomatic behaviour' if they responded positively to 2 or more of the relevant statements and those who responded positively to the statement on binge drinking were defined as 'binge drinkers'. However, adults who satisfied the conditions for any one of these three components may not have met the criteria for being defined as alcohol dependent.

The private household survey also considered alcohol problems. However, corresponding data were not collected this survey as many of the questions were not appropriate for those resident in institutions.

Drug use

Informants were asked about their use of drugs including sedatives, tranquillisers, cannabis, amphetamines, cocaine, heroin, opiates, hallucinogens, Ecstasy and glue. Report 5 covers medical use of prescribed drugs, most usually sedatives and tranquillisers; in this report we were only interested in their extra-medical use.

Extra-medical and illicit use was ascertained by presenting informants with a list of drugs and asking if they had used any of these without a prescription, or more than was prescribed for them, or to get high. Sedatives and tranquillisers were placed highest on the list to deter adults who did not use illicit drugs but did misuse medication from assuming the questions did not apply to them.

List of commonly used drugs

Sleeping pills, Barbiturates, Sedatives, Downers, Seconal

Tranquillisers, Valium, Lithium

Cannabis, Marijuana, Hash, Dope, Grass, Ganja, Kif

Amphetamines, Speed, Uppers, Stimulants, Qat

Cocaine, Coke, Crack

Heroin, Smack

Opiates other than heroin: Demerol, Morphine, Methadone, Darvon, Opium, DF118

Psychedelics, Hallucinogens: LSD, Mescaline, Acid, Peyote, Psilocybin (magic) mushrooms

Ecstasy

Solvents, Inhalants, Glue, Amyl nitrate

The questions on drug use and the drug categories were drawn form the drugs section of the Diagnostic Interview Schedule (DIS)[15] and were used in the U.S. ECA study[16]. Questions on injecting drugs and needle sharing were added.

Informants who reported using any of the drugs listed either without a prescription, or at more than the prescibed dosage, or to get high, were then asked if they had taken the drug more than five times in their life. Those who had done so and had also taken the drug in the past twelve months were defined as users of the drug.

Cigarette smoking

All informants, except proxies, were asked if they had ever smoked cigarettes, and if they smoked nowadays. This did not include cigar and pipe smoking. If they did smoke, they were asked how many cigarettes they smoked a day. This was prompted firstly for weekdays, and then for weekends to get a more accurate average daily consumption. Adults were grouped into categories, depending on whether they had ever smoked, and the average daily amount smoked.

Cigarette smoking categories

Never regularly smoked	
Ex-smokers	
Current smokers:	
Light	Less than 10 a day
Moderate	Less than 20 a day, but more than 10
Heavy	More than 20 a day

The questions asked were identical to those in the 1992 General Household Survey (GHS)[17] and the 1993 Health Survey for England[18], although neither of these surveys covered people living in institutions.

Other reports on the institution survey

Report 4

Report 4[19] presents the prevalence of mental disorders in the institutional population. It shows that prevalence of disorders (based on ICD-10 chapters) varies according to type of institution. Characteristics of the institutions are provided. Two tables from this report showing the proportions of residents with each type of disorder by type of institution are shown on pages xviii and xix.

Report 4 also includes information on the survey methodology: the sample design, response, and the method used to weight the data. The questionnaires used in the survey are printed as an Appendix to Report 4.

Report 5

Report 5 looks at the same three groups of residents as this report but focuses on their physical complaints, treatment, and use of services. Report 5 also provides more information on the personal characteristics of those in the three disorder groups, and on the characteristics of the institutions in which they were resident.

Proportions of residents with each type of disorder by type of hospital setting

		NHS psychiatric hospital	NHS unit/ward of general hospital	Private hospital, clinic or nursing home	All hospitals, clinics, or nursing homes
Primary diagnosis (based on ICD-10)		%	%	%	%
F00-F09	Organic mental disorders	4	1	1	2
F10-F19	Mental and behavioural disorders due to psychoactive substance use	0	0	0	0
F20-F29	Schizophrenia, delusional and schizoaffective disorders	75	81	61	72
F30-F39	Mood disorders excluding depressive episode: affective psychoses	7	10	24	14
F40-F48	Neurotic, stress-related and somatoform disorders including depressive episode	4	3	4	4
F50-F59	Behavioural syndromes associated with psychological disturbances and physical factors	0	2	5	2
F60-F69	Disorders of adult personality and behaviour	1	0	0	0
F70-F79	Mental retardation	0	0	0	0
F80-F89	Disorders of psychological development	0	0	3	1
F90-F98	Behavioural and emotional disorders with onset usually occurring in childhood and adolescence	0	0	0	0
	Insufficient information	6	3	0	3
	No answer / refusal	1	0	1	0
Base (all residents)		*341*	*66*	*80*	*487*

Proportions of residents with each type of disorder by type of residential accommodation

		Residential care home	Group home	Hostels	Ordinary/ recognised housing	All residential accommodation
Primary diagnosis (based on ICD-10)		%	%	%	%	%
F00-F09	Organic mental disorders	1	0	0	0	0
F10-F19	Mental and behavioural disorders due to psychoactive substance use	1	1	0	2	1
F20-F29	Schizophrenia, delusional and schizoaffective disorders	65	68	58	76	67
F30-F39	Mood disorders excluding depressive episode: affective psychoses	7	9	3	6	6
F40-F48	Neurotic, stress-related and somatoform disorders including depressive episode	11	11	19	7	12
F50-F59	Behavioural syndromes associated with psychological disturbances and physical factors	1	0	0	0	0
F60-F69	Disorders of adult personality and behaviour	1	1	0	0	0
F70-F79	Mental retardation	0	0	0	0	0
F80-F89	Disorders of psychological development	2	0	2	2	2
F90-F98	Behavioural and emotional disorders with onset usually occurring in childhood and adolescence	0	0	0	0	0
	Insufficient information	10	8	16	6	10
	No answer / refusal	1	3	2	1	2
Base (all residents)		*297*	*166*	*125*	*94*	*705*

Notes and references

1   The institutional survey involved interviews with about 1200 randomly sampled residents in Great Britain. In addition to this survey, interviews were also conducted in private households and accommodation specifically catering for homeless people.

2   Data for secondary analysis can be obtained from the ESRC data archive at the University of Essex. Independent researchers should apply to:

Ms Kathy Sayer
ESRC Data Archive
University of Essex
Wivenhoe Park
Colchester
Essex CO4 3SQ

Tel (UK) 01206 872323
Fax (UK) 01206 872003
Email: archive@: Essex.AC.UK

3   Lewis, G., Pelosi, A.J. and Dunn, G., (1992) Measuring Psychiatric disorder in the community: a standardized assessment for use by lay interviewers, Psychological Medicine, **22**, 465-486

4   Brewin, C.R and Wing, J.K., (1989) MRC Needs for Care assessment, MRC Social Psychiatry Unit, Institute of Psychiatry, London.

5   Martin, J., Meltzer, H., and Elliot, D. (1988) The OPCS Surveys of Disability in Great Britain, Report 1, The prevalence of disability among adults, HMSO, London.

6   Meltzer, H., Gill, B., Petticrew, M., and Hinds, K., (1995) *OPCS Surveys of Psychiatric Morbidity in Great Britain, Report 3: Economic activity and social functioning of adults with psychiatric disorders*. HMSO: London, Chapter 2

7   *The Health and Lifestyle Survey*, Health Promotion Research Trust, 1987

8   Brugha, T.S. et al (1993) The relationship of social network deficits with deficits in social functioning in long–term psychiatric disorders. *Social Psychiatry and Psychiatric Epidemiology*, **28**, 218–224

9   Brugha et al (1987). The Interview Measure of Social Relationships: the description and evaluation of a survey instrument for assessing personal social resources. *Social Psychiatry*, **22**, 123–128

10 Meltzer, H., Gill, B., Hinds, K., and Petticrew, M., (1996) *OPCS Surveys of Psychiatric Morbidity in Great Britain, Report 5: Physical complaints, service use and treatment of residents with psychiatric disorders*, HMSO: London

11 Meltzer, H., Gill, B., Petticrew, M., and Hinds, K., (1995) *OPCS Surveys of Psychiatric Morbidity in Great Britain, Report 3: Economic activity and social functioning of adults with psychiatric disorders*. HMSO: London, Chapter 5

12 Thomas, M. et al (1994) *1992 General Household Survey*. HMSO: London

13 Bennett, N et al (1995) *Health Survey for England 1993*. HMSO: London

14 *Alcohol and the heart in perspective: sensible limits reaffirmed*. Report of a joint working group of the Royal College of Physicians, the Royal College of Psychiatrists and the Royal College of General Practitioners. June 1995

15 Robins, L.N., Helzer, J.E., Croughan, J. and Ratcliff, K.S., (1981) National Institute of Mental Health Diagnostic Interview Schedule: Its History, Characteristics, and Validity, *Archives of General Psychiatry*, **38**, pp 381–389

16 *Psychiatric Disorders in America. The
    Epidemiologic Catchment Area Study,*
    edited by Robins, L.N., and Reiger, D.A.,
    (1991) Free Press, New York

17 1992 General Household Survey op. cit.

18 Health Survey for England 1993 op. cit.

19 Meltzer, H., Gill, B., Petticrew, M., and
    Hinds, K., (1995) *OPCS Surveys of
    Psychiatric Morbidity in Great Britain,
    Report 4: the prevalence of psychiatric
    morbidity among adults living in
    institutions*, HMSO: London

Summary of main findings

In 1994, 70% of adults aged 16-64 permanently resident in institutions in Great Britain that cater for people with mental health problems suffered from schizophrenia, delusional and schizoaffective disorders. About 8% suffered from affective psychosis (mainly bipolar affective disorder), 8% had neurotic disorders, and 5% had other mental disorders. For the remaining 9% there was insufficient information to categorise residents.

Each of the three chapters in this Report is devoted to a particular group of residents: those with schizophrenia, delusional or schizoaffective disorders (Chapter 1); residents who have affective psychosis (Chapter 2), and those classified as having a neurotic disorder (Chapter 3). In this Summary we highlight, for each group, the main differences in residents' economic circumstances, difficulties with activities of daily living, social functioning, and use of alcohol, drugs and tobacco by type of institution. Data from all three chapters are also brought together to compare the characteristics of residents by type of disorder.

Residents with schizophrenia

- Just under three quarters of all residents who had schizophrenia were permanently unable to work (71%); the proportion was slightly lower among those in ordinary housing/ recognised lodging (63%).

- Under half of all residents with schizophrenia (43%) controlled their own finances; the proportions doing so ranged from 31% of those in hospitals, to 82% of those in group homes.

- About three quarters of those in residential care homes and ordinary housing/recognised lodging received Income Support.

- The difficulty most likely to be reported was dealing with paperwork which was problematic for over half of those in each type of residential accommodation.

- Residents with schizophrenia felt lacking in social support. Fewer than a quarter perceived no lack of social support while 43% reported a severe lack.

- Nine per cent of residents with schizophrenia had no close friends or relatives, in or out of the establishment.

- The proportion of residents who had primary support groups of 3 adults or fewer ranged from 23% among hostel residents to 36% among those in residential care homes.

- Almost a quarter of residents (24%) attended day centres, ranging from 8% of those in hospital to 47% of those living in hostels.

- 13% of men and 1% of women reported drinking more than the recommended sensible level.

- Three quarters of residents with schizophrenia smoked cigarettes: 55% of men, and 39% of women, were classified as heavy smokers.

Residents with affective psychoses

- Over half the residents with affective psychoses were permanently unable to work (55%); the proportion ranged from 65% of those in hospitals to 44% of those in residential accommodation.

- Among those in hospitals a third controlled their own finances compared with three quarters of residents with affective psychosis living in residential accommodation.

- Half of those living in residential accommodation had difficulty with paperwork..

- A quarter of residents with affective psychoses perceived no lack of social support; 43% perceived a severe lack of social support and a further 30% had a moderate lack.

- 15% had no close relatives outside of the establishment.

- Heavy drinking was more prevalent in hospitals than in residential accommodation, and particularly among men .

- Eighteen per cent of residents with affective psychoses were defined as drug users, with the proportion considerably higher among those in residential accommodation compared with those in hospitals.

- Half the residents with affective psychoses were heavy cigarette smokers.

Residents with neurotic disorders

- Just over half of residents with neurotic disorders were permanently unable to work (52%).

- Almost two thirds (63%) of those with neurotic disorders controlled their own finances.

- Half the residents reported difficulty with paperwork and a quarter had problems with each of managing money and using transport.

- Forty three per cent of residents with neurotic disorders perceived a severe lack of social support and a further 20% had a moderate lack.

- Almost two thirds (64%) had no more than 2 close friends outside of their establishments.

- Forty one per cent of those with neurotic disorders were non-, or occasional drinkers, while 14% drank more than the recommended sensible level.

- Just under a quarter (22%) of residents with neurotic disorders had used some drug; 11% had taken cannabis, 8% tranquillisers and 6% sleeping tablets.

- Three quarters of residents with neurotic disorders were light, moderate or heavy cigarette smokers; the majority smoked heavily (46% of men and 24% of women).

Economic functioning by type of disorder

Most residents of institutions were permanently unable to work. Those with schizophrenia were most likely to be in this position (71%) compared with just over half of those with other

Summary Table 1 Economic and financial characteristics by type of disorder

	Schizophrenia, delusional or schizoaffective disorders	Affective psychoses	Neurotic disorders
	Percentage of residents who:		
Were permanently unable to work*	71	55	52
Were working*	12	16	13
Controlled their own finances*	43	55	63
Received any social security benefits**	96	97	81
Had any additional income**	20	36	36
Base	*828*/ 218***	*96*/ 33***	*101*/ 56***

* Data available for all adults. See first Base

** Data available only for those who controlled their own finances, and not for adults in hospitals. See second Base

disorders. Many residents did not control their own finances; only 43% of those with schizophrenia did so, with the proportions rising to 55% and 63% of those with affective psychosis and neurotic disorders respectively. As shown in subsequent chapters type of institution was strongly associated with control of finances.

Data on receipt of benefits were only asked of adults who were not resident in hospitals. While almost all of those with schizophrenia and affective psychosis who were not in hospitals received some social security benefits, only 81% of those with neurotic disorders did.

Social functioning by type of disorder

The proportion of adults perceiving a severe lack of social support did not vary by disorder (43%).

Whereas 7% of adults in private households had primary support groups (comprising adults they felt close to) of three or fewer, up to 30% of those in institutions had correspondingly limited primary support groups.

Adults with affective psychosis were more active than residents with other disorders. Again type of institution was strongly associated with participation in leisure activities.

Summary Table 2   Social functioning by type of disorder: a comparison with the sample from the Private Household Survey

	Residents with schizophrenia, delusional or schizoaffective disorders	Residents with affective psychoses	Residents with neurotic disorders	All adults in Private Household Survey
Percentage of residents who:				
Perceived severe lack of social support*	43	43	44	9
Had a primary support group of 3 or fewer adults*	30	18	30	7
Had no close friends or relatives*	9	4	2	-
Were involved in 3 or fewer leisure activities**	29	16	34	6
Base	*588*/ 828**	*68*/ 96**	*99*/ 101**	*9741*

*   Data available for subject interviews only. See first Base

** Data available for all adults. See second Base

Use of alcohol, drugs and tobacco by type of disorder

Although there was some variation regarding drinking alcohol, misusing drugs, and smoking cigarettes among the institutional population according to disorder, these were far less striking than variations between this group as a whole and the private household population.

While only 20% of those in private households did not drink alcohol, or did so only occasionally, among those in institutions the proportions abstaining were more than double this. Twenty two per cent of the private household sample were found to be drinking more than the recommended sensible weekly level ('Heavy'

drinkers); this was double the proportion among residents of institutions. Of course there was some variation within disorder groups according to the type of institutions in which residents were living. For example, it is interesting to note that in Chapter 1, the highest proportion of heavy drinkers with schizophrenia was found in hospitals (15%) and the lowest in hostels (2%).

While only 11% of the private household population were heavy smokers (rising to 18% of those identified as having a neurotic disorder), among those in institutions about half of those with schizophrenia and affective psychosis smoked heavily and 41% of those with neurotic disorders did so.

Summary Table 3   **Alcohol, drug and tobacco use by type of disorder : a comparison with the sample from the Private Household Survey**

	Residents with schizophrenia, delusional or or schizoaffective disorders	Residents with affective psychoses	Residents with neurotic disorders	All adults in Private Household Survey
Percentage of residents who:				
Were abstainers or occasional drinkers	49	56	40	20
Were heavy drinkers	10	10	14	22
Used any drug	7	18	22	5
Used cannabis	5	8	11	5
Used hypnotics	2	10	12	1
Were heavy smokers	51	49	41	11
Never smoked regularly	17	26	11	47
Base	*588*	*68*	*99*	*9741*

Data available for subject interviews only

1 Residents with schizophrenia, delusional or schizoaffective disorders

1.1 Introduction

This chapter focuses on those residents living in institutions who had schizophrenia, delusional or schizoaffective disorders; the shorthand 'residents with schizophrenia' is used to describe this group. The diagnosis of schizophrenia was based on self-report, or given by staff (as described in the focus of the report). Because no clinical assessment was made by the interviewing team in arriving at this broad diagnostic category, residents could not be further classified as having either schizophrenia, a delusional disorder or a schizoaffective disorder. Although interviewers carried out a CIS-R interview, this does not cover psychosis; SCAN interviews were not carried out in the institutions survey[1].

The chapter begins with a descriptive profile of residents and then presents information on their economic activity, on difficulties with activities of daily living and on their social functioning. The use of alcohol, drugs and tobacco is finally analysed. Details about the various measures used in the analysis are given in the *focus of the report*.

Proxy informants

Sixty five per cent of the sample of residents with schizophrenia were themselves interviewed for the survey, and a further 6% were interviewed in conjunction with another person. For 29% a subject interview was not obtained, and information was collected by proxy. Some questions (including the CIS-R) were not suitable for proxy informants. Therefore, data on certain topics (for example, perceived social support, use of alcohol, drugs and tobacco) are only available for 588 of the 828 residents with schizophrenia (71%).

1.2 Descriptive profile of residents

Information on the personal characteristics of residents with schizophrenia and on the types of institutions in which they lived is covered in detail in Report 5 [2], however much of this information is also included here with very brief commentary for reference purposes and because characteristics of residents are used as explanatory variables. This section also provides some information on the characteristics of respondents interviewed by proxy.

Personal characteristics

Just under three quarters of all residents who had schizophrenia were men. Their average age was in the mid-forties and for the most part they were single, white men who had not obtained any educational qualifications. (*Table 1.1*)

Just under a quarter of residents (23%) reported having a longstanding physical complaint; nervous system and musculo-skeletal complaints were most prevalent, each affecting 6% of residents. (*Table 1.2*)

Institutional characteristics

Just under half (43%) of schizophrenics were resident in hospitals; just under a quarter (23%) were in residential care homes. Fourteen per cent lived in group homes and the remaining 18% were divided equally between hostels and ordinary housing/ recognised lodging. In subsequent sections of this chapter, data are analysed according to the type of institution in which residents lived. Personal characteristics are shown by type of institution in Table 1.3.

A higher proportion of interviews about residents with schizophrenia in hospitals were carried out by proxy than in other types of accommodation; for example, 40% of interviews in hospitals were conducted by proxy compared with 15% in group homes and hostels. Over three quarters of the proxy interviews in hospitals (78%) were carried out because residents were unable to be interviewed themselves due to their mental health problem. Although this was the main cause for proxy interviews in all settings, it was most significant in hospitals. Further information on the characteristics of residents who were interviewed themselves compared with those interviewed by proxy, is presented in Appendix B of this report.

The mean length of time residents with schizophrenia had been living at their present establishment was 5.3 years; the mean length of stay varied by type of institution, being highest in hospitals, 7.2 years. (*Table 1.4*)

Psychiatric characteristics

Some residents with schizophrenia were also identified as having neurotic disorders, however this was only possible if informants were able to respond to the CIS-R; 72% of residents with schizophrenia answered the CIS-R and 45% of these had some neurotic disorder. Of the 14 neurotic symptoms measured by the CIS-R, fatigue was most prevalent affecting 43% of residents who responded to the CIS-R. Around a third of residents had significant symptoms of sleep problems, worry and anxiety. (*Table 1.5*)

1.3 Economic functioning of residents

Just under three quarters of all residents who had schizophrenia were permanently unable to work due to long-term sickness or disability (71%). The proportion who were permanently not working was slightly lower among those in ordinary housing/ recognised lodging (63%). Twelve per cent of residents with schizophrenia reported that they were working, although this was not necessarily regular, paid employment. Within hospitals for example, residents

may have regarded themselves as working, if they were being paid for helping out in their institutions. (*Table 1.6*)

Under half of all residents with schizophrenia (43%) controlled their own finances; the proportions doing so ranged from 31% of those in hospitals, to 82% of those in group homes. Appointees such as friends or relatives were most likely to control the finances of those who delegated this responsibility. In residential care homes and ordinary housing/ recognised lodging, members of staff played a more significant role than appointees, controlling the finances of a quarter of residents. (*Table 1.7*)

Residents who controlled their own finances were asked about social security benefits they received, and about any other sources of income they had. These questions were not asked of those in hospitals. Over 90% of those in residential accommodation were receiving some benefits. About three quarters of those in residential care homes and ordinary housing/ recognised lodging received Income Support and 38% and 44% respectively received Invalidity Pensions. Among residents of group homes, 65% received Invalidity Pensions and 33% received Income Support. Disability Living Allowance was received by 12-29% of residents.

Fewer than a third (32%) of residents with schizophrenia living in group homes had any additional sources of income. Among those living in other types of residential accommodation the proportions were even lower (15% among those residing in ordinary housing/ recognised lodging and 11% of those living in residential care homes). Interest from savings was the major source of additional income. (*Table 1.8*)

1.4 Activities of daily living (ADL)

The difficulty most likely to be reported was dealing with paperwork, which was problematic for over half of those in each type of residential accommodation. Personal care was least likely to be a problem, proving difficult for fewer than one in five adults in any type of residential accommodation. At least two thirds of adults living in each type of residential accommodation reported some ADL difficulty. Among residents with schizophrenia in residential care homes, those with a physical health problem were more likely to have an ADL difficulty than those without (84% compared with 68%). Among those living in group homes, hostels and recognised lodgings no variations by physical complaints were found.

In each type of accommodation, the vast majority of residents needing help with ADLs received such help. The worst case of un-met need was found for those in ordinary housing/ recognised lodging where just 4% of adults needed, but did not receive, help with household activities.

The major providers of help were home careworkers, staff or owners of homes, landlords and social workers. Relatives and friends played some role, but even where they were most involved, (practical activities and managing money), they provided help for no more than 12% of residents receiving help. (*Tables 1.9 to 1.12*)

1.5 Social functioning of residents

Perceived social support

The data show that residents with schizophrenia felt lacking in social support. Fewer than a third perceived no lack of social support, while 43% reported a severe lack. As a measure of comparison, in the private household survey, only 9% of adults reported a severe lack of social support although this rose to 25% among those with the most severe neurotic disorder, depressive episode. There were no major variations in levels of self-perceived social support according to the type of institution. (*Table 1.13*)

Extent of social networks

Forty five per cent of residents in hospitals felt close to no-one in the establishment. This was higher than the corresponding proportions for those in the various types of residential accommodation (28%-39%), although this latter group were more likely than hospital residents to live alone (5%-21%).

Most residents with schizophrenia (three quarters) felt close to one or more relatives outside their establishment and just over half had one or more friends outside the institution whom they regarded as close. Only just over a quarter of residents with schizophrenia had more than two friends outside the establishment that they felt close to. Nine per cent of residents with schizophrenia had no close friends or relatives, in or out of the establishment.

The proportion of residents who had primary support groups of 3 adults or fewer ranged from 23% among hostel residents to 36% among those in residential care homes. (*Tables 1.14 and 1.15*)

Leisure activities

Residents with schizophrenia participated in a mean of three leisure activities in and around the establishment, and three outside it. The modal number of leisure activities outside the establishment was 0 for hospital residents, compared with 4 for those in residential care homes. Among the different accommodation types, hospitals had the highest proportion of residents who participated in a total of 3 activities or fewer, 35%. In other accommodation types, only a quarter of residents fell into this category.

In each of type of institution, by far the most popular activity was watching the TV or listening to the radio; this was a pastime for 86% of residents overall. Listening to music (69%) came next, followed by shopping (56%). (*Tables 1.16 and 1.17*)

Almost a quarter of residents (24%) attended day centres, ranging from 8% of those in hospital to 47% of those living in hostels. Sixteen percent of residents with schizophrenia attended clubs for people with mental health problems; 9% of those in hospitals, but over one in five of those in residential care homes, group homes or ordinary housing/ recognised lodging. Only 3% and 2% of residents with schizophrenia regularly went to an Adult Education Centre or an Adult Training Centre respectively. (*Table 1.18*)

1.6 Use of alcohol, drugs and tobacco

Alcohol consumption

Patterns of alcohol consumption among residents with schizophrenia varied more by sex than by type of institution. Overall 13% of men and 1% of women reported drinking more than the recommended sensible level. Alcohol consumption beyond this level was most prevalent in hospitals (14%) and group homes (12%) and least common in hostels (2%). There was also some variation by age, younger residents being more likely to abstain or drink only occasionally, than older residents. Alcohol dependence was recorded for two and three per cent of residents in hostels and hospitals respectively, and for 8%-10% among those in other types of accommodation. (*Tables 1.19 and 1.20*)

Drug use

Overall 7% of residents with schizophrenia reported having used some drug; this was true of 3% of those in ordinary housing/ recognised lodging, compared with 13% of those in group homes. Cannabis was most likely to be used (5%), then hypnotics (sleeping tablets and tranquillisers; 2%). (*Table 1.21*)

Two per cent of residents with schizophrenia who were interviewed said that they had injected themselves with drugs at some stage.

Cigarette smoking

This survey found that three quarters of residents with schizophrenia smoked cigarettes. In fact over half (55%) of men, and 39% of women, were classified as heavy smokers. (*Table 1.22*)

Almost two thirds of residents with schizophrenia who currently smoked said that they would find it very difficult not to smoke for a whole day (64%). Almost a third (30%) reported usually having their first cigarette of the day within 5 minutes of waking and only 12% waited for an hour or more before their first cigarette. Between 48% (hospitals) and 64% (group homes) of residents said that they would like to give up smoking cigarettes. (*Table 1.23*)

Data from the private household survey and other surveys suggested that the use of alcohol, drugs and tobacco were associated with each other. Table 1.24 compares the mean and median alcohol consumption for adults who did and did not smoke cigarettes. While the mean weekly consumption for non-smokers was 3.7 units, for smokers, it was more than twice this amount, at 8.2 units. (*Table 1.24*)

Notes and references

1. Lewis, G., Pelosi, A.J., and Dunn, G.,(1992) Measuring Psychiatric disorder in the community; a standardised assessment for use by interviewers, *Psychological Medicine,* **22**, 465–486

   Lewis, G., and Pelosi, A.J., *Manual of the Revised Clinical Interview Schedule (CIS–R)*, June 1990, MRC Institute of Psychiatry

2. Meltzer, H., Gill, B., Hinds, K., and Petticrew, M., (1996) *OPCS Surveys of Psychiatric Morbidity in Great Britain, Report 5: Physical complaints, service use and treatment of residents with psychiatric disorders.* HMSO: London

Table 1.1   Personal characteristics of residents by sex

Residents with schizophrenia, delusional or schizoaffective disorders

	Men	Women	All
	%	%	%
Age			
16-24	4	7	5
25-34	24	13	20
35-44	24	21	23
45-54	28	30	29
55-64	20	30	23
Marital status			
Married/cohabiting	2	8	3
Single	86	66	80
Widowed	1	4	2
Divorced	10	21	13
Separated	2	3	2
Ethnicity			
White or European	90	95	91
West Indian or African	7	3	6
Asian or Oriental	3	2	2
Other	1	0	1
Qualifications			
A level or higher	10	10	10
GCSE/O level	9	13	10
Other qualifications	8	7	8
No qualifications	72	70	72
Base	*586*	*242*	*828*
% of men and women with schizophrenia	71%	29%	100%

Table 1.2   Percentage of residents with each long standing physical complaint by sex

Residents with schizophrenia, delusional or schizoaffective disorders

	Men	Women	All
	Percentage with each complaint		
Nervous system complaints	**6**	**6**	**6**
Epilepsy	3	4	3
Huntington's chorea	1	1	1
Brain damage from infection/ injury	1	1	1
Parkinson's disease	0	0	0
Other nervous system complaints	1	0	1
Musculo-skeletal complaints	**4**	**10**	**6**
Arthritis/ rhematism/ fibrositis	2	4	2
Back and neck problems/ slipped disk	1	1	1
Other problems of bones/ muscles/ joints	2	6	3
Endocrine/ nutritional/ metabolic diseases and immunity disorders	**3**	**8**	**5**
Diabetes	3	4	3
Hyper- or hypo- thyroidism	0	4	1
Other complaints	0	1	1
Heart and circulatory system complaints	**4**	**5**	**4**
Cerebral haemorrhage	0	1	1
Heart attack/ angina	1	1	1
Hypertension	1	2	1
Other complaints	2	2	2
Genito-urinary system complaints	**0**	**2**	**1**
Respiratory system complaints	**2**	**1**	**2**
Digestive system complaints	**4**	**4**	**4**
Eye complaints	**1**	**2**	**1**
Ear complaints	**1**	**0**	**1**
Skin complaints	**2**	**2**	**2**
Neoplasms (and benign lumps or cysts)	**1**	**1**	**1**
Infectious and parasitic diseases	**0**	**0**	**0**
Blood disorders	**0**	**1**	**0**
Any physical complaint	**21**	**27**	**23**
Base	*586*	*242*	*828*

Table 1.3 Personal characteristics of residents by type of institution

Residents with schizophrenia, delusional or schizoaffective disorders

	Hospitals clinics and nursing homes	Residential care homes	Group homes	Hostels	Ordinary housing/ Recognised lodging	All*
	%	%	%	%	%	%
Sex						
Men	71	66	83	68	70	71
Women	29	34	17	32	30	29
Age						
16-34	31	23	18	24	13	25
35-44	20	22	22	37	28	23
45-54	27	33	34	24	22	29
55-64	22	21	25	16	37	23
Marital status						
Married/cohabiting	4	2	3	-	8	3
Single	79	82	80	81	77	80
Widowed	2	2	1	2	2	2
Divorced	13	14	12	15	10	13
Separated	2	1	3	2	3	2
Ethnicity						
White or European	89	92	95	93	92	91
West Indian or African	6	5	5	5	2	6
Asian or Oriental	4	2	-	-	2	2
Other	2	-	-	2	-	2
Qualifications						
A level or higher	8	8	15	20	15	10
GCSE/O level	9	12	13	6	17	10
Other qualifications	6	8	8	7	10	8
No qualifications	77	72	64	68	59	72
Base	*359*	*193*	*113*	*73*	*71*	*828*
% of adults with schizophrenia in each type of institution	**43%**	**23%**	**14%**	**9%**	**9%**	**100%**

* Includes 19 residents (2%) living in another type of residential accommodation

Table 1.4 Residence charateristics of residents by type of institution

Residents with schizophrenia, delusional or schizoaffective disorders

	Hospitals clinics & nursing homes	Residential care homes	Group homes	Hostels	Ordinary housing/ Recognised lodging	All*
	%	%	%	%	%	%
Length of stay						
Less than 1 year	21	23	17	23	10	20
1 year < 2 years	14	20	9	16	14	15
2 years < 3 years	19	14	14	14	16	17
3 years < 4 years	6	12	18	8	17	10
4 years < 5 years	5	6	12	18	8	8
5 years < 6 years	4	4	8	1	8	5
6 years < 7 years	1	5	2	2	0	2
7 years < 8 years	2	5	9	6	2	4
8 years < 9 years	3	2	5	4	6	3
9 years < 10 years	2	3	-	3	8	2
10 years < 15 years	6	4	7	5	9	6
15 years < 20 years	4	2	-	-	2	2
20 years < 25 years	3	-	-	-	-	1
25 years < 30 years	3	-	-	-	-	2
30 years < 35 years	4	-	-	-	-	2
35 years < 40 years	1	-	-	-	-	1
40 years or more	1	-	-	-	-	1
Mean length of stay (years)	7.2	3.6	4.2	3.6	4.8	5.3
(Mean age)	(46)	(44)	(46)	(43)	(48)	(44)
Median length of stay (years)	2.5	2.5	3.5	2.5	3.5	2.5
(Median age)	(44)	(46)	(47)	(41)	(49)	(45)
Where subject was living						
before present institution	%	%	%	%	%	%
Hospital, clinic or nursing home	38	44	30	32	46	39
Private household	45	30	26	25	21	35
Supported accommodation/ group home	5	4	20	13	26	10
Residential care home	1	17	16	20	3	9
Prison/ on remand	6	1	-	-	-	3
B&B/ Hotel/ Hostel	2	2	2	5	2	2
Sleeping rough	1	-	1	2	0	1
Other	2	2	4	2	1	2
Base	*359*	*193*	*113*	*73*	*71*	*828*

* Includes 19 residents living in another type of residential accommodation

Table 1.5 Neurotic disorders and significant neurotic symptoms (as measured by the CIS-R) by type of institution

Residents with schizophrenia, delusional and schizoaffective disorders who answered the CIS-R

	Hospitals clinics & nursing homes	Residential care homes	Group homes	Hostels	Ordinary housing/ Recognised lodging	All*
	%	%	%	%	%	%
Number of neurotic disorders						
0	52	58	54	46	66	55
1	34	28	28	47	26	31
2	9	10	14	5	6	10
3	4	4	1	2	2	3
4	0	-	1	-	-	0
Any neurotic disorder	**48**	**42**	**46**	**54**	**34**	**45**
Percentage with each neurotic disorder						
Type of neurotic disorder						
Generalised Anxiety Disorder	21	24	29	20	15	22
Mixed anxiety and depressive disorder	4	18	15	12	10	10
Depressive episode	11	7	10	8	2	8
Phobia	6	9	11	6	7	8
Obsessive-Compulsive Disorder	7	6	10	2	2	6
Panic	6	2	2	9	4	5
Percentage with each significant neurotic symptom						
Significant neurotic symptoms						
Fatigue	47	44	44	55	24	43
Sleep problems	36	35	51	20	31	36
Worry	33	34	43	34	28	34
Anxiety	32	32	39	28	20	32
Concentration/forgetfulness	30	32	30	29	17	28
Depression	28	22	26	26	8	24
Depressive ideas	25	28	27	27	13	24
Obsessions	22	22	25	11	25	20
Irritability	22	19	19	21	16	20
Compulsions	23	10	24	16	19	18
Phobia	12	21	16	12	16	16
Panic	21	15	15	10	11	16
Worry about physical health	17	17	20	12	10	16
Somatic symptoms	19	11	11	12	10	13
Base	*220*	*147*	*96*	*59*	*59*	*596*

* Includes 14 residents living in another type of residential accommodation

Table 1.6   Economic activity by type of institution

Residents with schizophrenia, delusional or schizoaffective disorders

Economic activity	Hospitals clinics & nursing homes	Residential care homes	Group homes	Hostels	Ordinary housing/ Recognised lodging	All*
	%	%	%	%	%	%
Permanently unable to work	73	71	72	75	63	71
Working	10	12	11	12	14	12
Intending to look, temporarily sick	3	4	2	4	6	5
Looking for work	1	4	6	-	6	3
Retired	1	1	1	-	2	1
Other	11	8	8	9	9	9
Base	*359*	*193*	*113*	*73*	*71*	*828*

* Includes 19 residents living in another type of residential accommodation

Table 1.7   Control of financial affairs by type of institution

Residents with schizophrenia, delusional or schizoaffective disorders

Who controls finances? *	Hospitals clinics and nursing homes	Residential care homes	Group homes	Hostels	Ordinary housing/ Recognised lodging	All**
	Percentage with finances controlled by:					
Self	31	38	82	36	56	43
Appointee (eg relative, friend)	51	19	11	41	12	32
Member of staff	11	29	7	18	25	17
DSS direct payments	4	11	-	5	2	5
Court of protection	2	3	-	-	2	2
Bank	2	1	-	-	10	2
Power of (enduring) attorney	0	1	-	-	2	1
Other	0	1	-	4	2	1
Base	*359*	*193*	*113*	*73*	*71*	*828*

* Adults who did not control their own financial affairs could have more than one alternative source of control

** Includes 19 residents living in another type of residential accommodation

Table 1.8 Receipt of benefits, and other sources of income, among adults controlling their own finances by type of institution

Residents with schizophrenia, delusional or schizoaffective disorders who controlled their own finances*

Social security benefits and other sources of income received	Residential care homes	Group homes	Hostels	Ordinary housing/ Recognised lodging
	Percentage receiving:			
Social security benefits				
Income support	76	33	[19]	74
Invalidity pension	44	65	[13]	38
Disability living allowance	12	27	[3]	29
N.I sickness benefit	12	10	[1]	11
Severe disablement allowance	7	7	[4]	15
Mobility allowance	2	2	[1]	4
Attendance allowance	1	2	[0]	4
Other benefits **	4	8	[1]	15
Receiving any benefits	**99**	**92**	**[24]**	**96**
Receiving no benefits	**1**	**8**	**[1]**	**4**
Other sources of income				
Interest from saving, investments etc	5	20	[4]	8
Earned income	4	10	[5]	7
Other regular allowances eg alimony	0	2	[2]	0
Income from self-employment	0	0	[0]	0
Pension from former employer	1	2	[0]	0
Any other source	0	2	[0]	0
Any additional income	**11**	**32**	**[9]**	**15**
No additional income	**89**	**68**	**[16]**	**85**
Base	*65*	*88*	*25*	*40*

* Data not available for adults who did not control their own finances; residents in hospitals were not asked about social security benefits or other sources of income

** including old age benefits, war widows pension and other benefits

Table 1.9 Number of ADL difficulties by type of institution

Residents with schizophrenia, delusional or schizoaffective disorders*

Number of ADL difficulties	Residential care home	Group homes	Hostels	Ordinary housing/ Recognised lodging
	%	%	%	%
0	28	33	24	32
1	32	29	22	12
2	17	9	22	16
3	5	7	22	10
4	6	12	3	12
5+	13	10	7	18
Base	*193*	*113*	*73*	*71*

* These data were not collected for adults in hospital

10

Table 1.10   Activities of daily living difficulties by type of institution and physical complaint

*Residents with schizophrenia, delusional or schizoaffective disorders **

Type of difficulty	Whether problem homes	Residential care	Group homes	Hostels	Ordinary housing/ Recognised lodging
		%	%	%	%
Physical complaint					
Dealing with paperwork	problem	50	51	[7]	[11]
	not problem	42	49	[2]	[6]
	does not apply	8	-	[3]	[1]
Managing money	problem	32	22	[2]	[6]
	not problem	54	78	[6]	[10]
	does not apply	14	-	[6]	[2]
Household activities	problem	31	39	[2]	[7]
	not problem	32	61	[8]	[10]
	does not apply	37	-	[3]	[1]
Medical care	problem	22	14	[5]	[3]
	not problem	78	86	[9]	[15]
	does not apply	-	-	[-]	[0]
Use of transport	problem	40	11	[4]	[5]
	not problem	60	89	[10]	[14]
	does not apply	-	-	-	-
Practical activities	problem	6	23	-	[5]
	not problem	21	43	[4]	[7]
	does not apply	73	35	[10]	[5]
Personal care	problem	27	10	[4]	[4]
	not problem	73	90	[10]	[15]
	does not apply	-	-	-	-
Difficulty with any of the above		**84**	**62**	**[12]**	**[14]**
Base		*48*	*36*	*15*	*19*

* These data were not collected for adults in hospitals

Table 1.10   Activities of daily living difficulties by type of institution and physical complaint
          continued

*Residents with schizophrenia, delusional or schizoaffective disorders ***

Type of difficulty	Whether problem	Residential care homes	Group homes	Hostels	Ordinary housing/ Recognised lodging
		%	%	%	%
No physical complaint					
Dealing with paperwork	problem	55	57	60	55
	not problem	42	43	35	38
	does not apply	3	-	5	7
Managing money	problem	37	26	43	38
	not problem	58	73	43	56
	does not apply	5	1	14	6
Household activities	problem	22	34	14	37
	not problem	70	66	67	52
	does not apply	8	-	20	11
Medical care	problem	26	18	47	38
	not problem	72	82	53	62
	does not apply	2	-	-	-
Use of transport	problem	17	20	5	19
	not problem	83	80	95	81
	does not apply	-	-	-	-
Practical activities	problem	19	17	8	28
	not problem	51	51	41	52
	does not apply	30	32	51	21
Personal care	problem	11	12	15	14
	not problem	89	88	85	86
	does not apply	-	-	-	-
Difficulty with any of the above		**68**	**69**	**75**	**67**
Base		*145*	*76*	*58*	*53*

* These data were not collected for adults in hospitals

Table 1.10 Activities of daily living difficulties by type of institution and physical complaint
continued

Residents with schizophrenia, delusional or schizoaffective disorders *

Type of difficulty	Whether problem	Residential care homes	Group homes	Hostels	Ordinary housing/ Recognised lodging
		%	%	%	%
All adults					
Dealing with paperwork	problem	54	55	60	56
	not problem	42	45	32	37
	does not apply	5	-	8	7
Managing money	problem	36	24	37	36
	not problem	57	75	44	56
	does not apply	8	1	19	8
Household activities	problem	24	36	14	37
	not problem	59	64	66	53
	does not apply	16	-	20	10
Medical care	problem	25	16	45	32
	not problem	74	84	55	67
	does not apply	1	-	-	0
Use of transport	problem	23	17	9	21
	not problem	77	83	91	79
	does not apply	-	-	-	-
Practical activities	problem	15	19	6	28
	not problem	43	48	38	49
	does not apply	42	33	56	23
Personal care	problem	15	12	18	16
	not problem	85	88	82	84
	does not apply	-	-	-	-
Difficulty with any of the above		**72**	**67**	**76**	**68**
Base		*193*	*113*	*73*	*71*

* These data were not collected for adults in hospitals

Table 1.11 Need for help by type of ADL difficulty by type of institution

*Residents with schizophrenia, delusional or schizoaffective disorders **

Type of difficulty	Residential care homes	Group home	Hostel	Ordinary housing/ Recognised lodging
	%	%	%	%
Dealing with paperwork				
Has difficulty, needs help, gets help	50	49	58	51
Has difficulty, needs help, gets no help	2	1	-	2
Has difficulty, needs no help	2	4	1	4
Has no difficulty	42	46	33	37
Does not apply	5	-	8	7
Managing money				
Has difficulty, needs help, gets help	33	21	35	34
Has difficulty, needs help, gets no help	-	1	1	-
Has difficulty, needs no help	2	3	-	2
Has no difficulty	57	75	45	56
Does not apply	8	1	19	8
Household activities				
Has difficulty, needs help, gets help	24	28	12	31
Has difficulty, needs help, gets no help	-	1	-	4
Has difficulty, needs no help	1	6	3	2
Has no difficulty	59	64	66	53
Does not apply	16	-	20	10
Medical care				
Has difficulty, needs help, gets help	25	14	41	32
Has difficulty, needs help, gets no help	-	-	1	-
Has difficulty, needs no help	-	1	-	-
Has no difficulty	74	85	57	67
Does not apply	1	-	-	0
Use of transport				
Has difficulty, needs help, gets help	17	11	9	10
Has difficulty, needs help, gets no help	-	-	-	-
Has difficulty, needs no help	6	6	-	11
Has no difficulty	77	83	91	79
Does not apply	-	-	-	-
Practical activities				
Has difficulty, needs help, gets help	14	15	6	24
Has difficulty, needs help, gets no help	-	1	-	-
Has difficulty, needs no help	1	3	-	4
Has no difficulty	43	48	38	49
Does not apply	42	33	56	23
Personal care				
Has difficulty, needs help, gets help	12	6	16	13
Has difficulty, needs help, gets no help	-	-	-	-
Has difficulty, needs no help	3	5	2	3
Has no difficulty	85	88	82	84
Does not apply	-	-	-	-
Difficulty with any of the above	72	67	76	68
Base	*193*	*113*	*73*	*71*

* These data were not collected for adults in hospitals

Table 1.12 Type of help by type of difficulty

Residents with schizophrenia, delusional or schizoaffective disorders*

Who gave help	Help received with						
	Dealing with paperwork	Managing money	Medical care	Household activities	Practical activities	Use of transport	Personal care
	Percentage receiving help from each source:						
Home careworker	32	32	38	48	29	42	60
Staff/ owner of home	23	29	22	26	30	22	16
Social worker	22	12	5	5	2	29	11
Landlord/ landlady	12	12	14	10	14	16	17
CPN/ Nurse	6	3	37	1	-	2	-
Occupational Therapist	1	1	-	-	-	-	-
Paid domestic help	0	0	1	2	-	-	1
Solicitor	1	-	-	-	-	-	-
Friend	6	4	1	7	7	14	11
Other residents	1	-	-	1	2	-	3
Parent	1	4	1	4	7	4	3
Spouse/ cohabitee	0	1	-	-	-	-	-
Brother/ sister	1	5	-	1	5	-	-
Son/ daughter	0	-	-	1	-	-	-
Boyfriend/ girlfriend	1	-	-	1	2	-	-
Any relative	4	10	1	6	12	6	3
Base	*222*	*133*	*109*	*102*	*61*	*55*	*51*

* These data were not collected for adults in hospitals

Table 1.13 Perceived social support by type of institution

Residents with schizophrenia, delusional or schizoaffective disorders*

Level of perceived social support	Hospitals clinics and nursing homes	Residential care homes	Group homes	Hostels	Ordinary housing/ Recognised lodging	All**
	%	%	%	%	%	%
No lack	20	20	26	23	33	23
Moderate lack	24	16	23	31	19	22
Severe lack	41	53	42	34	44	43
Unclassified	16	10	9	13	4	11
Base	*215*	*142*	*96*	*62*	*60*	*588*

*   Data available for subject interviews only

** Includes 14 residents living in another type of residential accommodation

Table 1.14   Extent of social networks by type of institution

Residents with schizophrenia, delusional or schizoaffective disorders*

Type and size of social network	Hospitals clinics and nursing homes	Residential care homes	Group homes	Hostels	Ordinary housing/ Recognised lodging	All**
	%	%	%	%	%	%
Co-residents and staff members that feel close to:***						
0	45	34	39	28	29	38
1	18	14	34	9	24	19
2	16	5	12	20	18	13
3	4	8	3	10	2	5
4 or more	16	32	6	28	6	19
Live alone	1	6	7	5	21	6
Relatives that don't live with, that feel close to: ***						
0	26	30	18	20	26	25
1	14 (62)	25 (75)	20 (58)	28 (58)	17 (59)	19 (63)
2	22	19	20	11	15	19
3	14	4	13	12	18	12
4	7	7	10	6	4	7
5	5	6	3	8	9	6
6	2	1	4	4	2	2
7	2	2	3	4	2	3
8	2	2	-	6	5	2
9	2	-	2	2	-	1
10 or more	4	2	7	-	0	4
Friends outside of household that feel close to: ***						
0	49	46	32	46	39	44
1	12 (73)	21 (80)	18 (62)	23 (71)	16 (66)	17 (71)
2	12	13	12	2	11	11
3	6	3	11	7	9	6
4	7	-	6	9	12	6
5	4	8	4	3	4	5
6	1	2	4	6	5	3
7	2	1	-	-	2	1
8	2	2	-	2	0	2
9	0	-	-	-	-	0
10	2	-	8	-	-	2
11	-	-	-	-	-	0
12	2	-	2	2	-	1
13 or more	1	3	2	-	0	1
Percentage of adults with no close friends or relatives	10	13	4	9	7	9
Base	*215*	*142*	*96*	*62*	*60*	*588*

*   Data avalable for subject interviews only

**   Includes 14 residents living in another type of residential accommodation

*** Percentages within each group total 100%

Table 1.15   Size of primary support group by type of institution

*Residents with schizophrenia, delusional or schizoaffective disorders**

Size of primary support group	Hospitals clinics and nursing homes	Residential Care homes	Group homes	Hostels	Ordinary housing/ Recognised lodging	All**
	%	%	%	%	%	%
9 or more	22	24	12	36	13	22
4 - 8	45	40	63	41	60	48
0 - 3	33	36	24	23	27	30
Base	*215*	*142*	*96*	*62*	*60*	*588*

*   Data available for subject interviews only

** Includes 14 residents living in another type of residential accommodation

Table 1.16   Use of leisure time by type of institution

Residents with schizophrenia, delusional or schizoaffective disorders

Use of leisure time	Hospitals clinics and nursing homes	Residential care homes	Group homes	Hostels	Ordinary housing/ Recognised lodging	All*
Number of activities involved in						
mean in and around the establishment	2.6	2.5	2.3	2.6	2.7	2.6
mode in and around the establishment	2	3	2	2	3	2
mean outside the establishment	2.7	3.2	3.0	3.1	4.1	3.1
mode outside the establishment	0	4	3	2	3	3
mean total	5.3	5.6	5.3	5.7	6.8	5.6
modal total	2	6	6	3	6	6
	%	%	%	%	%	%
Total number of activities						
0 - 3	35	25	25	29	21	29
4 - 9	50	63	66	58	55	56
10 or more	14	12	9	13	24	14
Base	*359*	*193*	*113*	*73*	*71*	*828*

* Includes 19 residents living in another type of residential accommodation

Table 1.17 Leisure activities by type of institution

Residents with schizophrenia, delusional and schizoaffective disorders

Leisure activities	Hospitals clinics and	Residential care homes	Group homes	Hostels	Ordinary housing/ Recognised lodging	All*
Percentage participating in each activity:						
In and around establishment						
TV/ radio	83	86	84	94	95	86
Listening to music	71	63	66	81	61	69
Reading books and newspapers	48	50	43	49	57	49
Writing letters/ telephoning	34	33	37	24	28	33
Games	32	32	11	31	15	28
Entertaining friends or relatives	30	23	25	20	34	27
Hobbies	23	27	27	28	39	26
Gardening	8	12	17	20	20	12
DIY/ car maintenance	1	2	1	0	8	2
Any activity	94	94	91	100	99	95
No activity	6	6	9	0	1	5
Out of the establishment						
Shopping	52	55	58	55	73	56
Going for a walk, walking the dog	44	53	39	55	57	48
Pubs, restaurants	41	53	47	38	54	46
Visiting friends or relatives	39	48	50	37	56	44
Cinema, theatre, concerts	18	22	15	19	36	21
Church	16	17	17	18	22	17
Sports as a participant	16	16	10	16	22	16
Library	10	13	15	12	18	12
Clubs, organisations	5	11	15	14	12	9
Sports as a spectator	8	7	6	16	10	9
Bingo, amusement arcades	4	10	4	9	10	7
Night clubs, discos	5	6	4	0	5	5
Bookmakers, betting and gambling	3	4	7	0	11	5
Classes, lectures	3	1	4	7	17	4
Political activities	0	0	0	0	4	0
Any activity	78	90	86	96	99	86
No activity	22	10	14	4	1	14
Base	*359*	*193*	*113*	*73*	*71*	*828*

* Includes 19 residents living in another type of residential accommodation

Table 1.18 Attendance at social, training, or educational centres by type of institution

Residents with schizophrenia, delusional or schizoaffective disorders

	Hospitals clinics and nursing homes	Residential care homes	Group homes	Hostels	Ordinary housing/ Recognised lodging	All*
	Percentage attending each type of centre					
Day centre	8	33	36	47	36	24
Club for people with mental health problems	9	21	21	13	27	16
Club for people with physical health problems	1	3	4	-	2	2
Adult education centre	2	2	5	7	2	3
Adult training centre	2	2	7	-	2	2
Base	*359*	*193*	*113*	*73*	*71*	*828*

* Includes 19 residents living in another type of residential accommodation

Table 1.19   Alcohol consumption by sex and type of institution; alcohol dependence by type of institution

*Residents with schizophrenia, delusional or schizoaffective disorders**

Alcohol consumption level	Hospitals clinics and nursing homes	Residential	Group homes	Hostels	Ordinary housing/ Recognised lodging	All**
	%	%	%	%	%	%
Women						
Abstainer***	46	21	[4]	[5]	[9]	32
Occasional drinker	37	39	[5]	[7]	[9]	35
(Abstainer + Occasional)	84	60	[9]	[12]	[18]	68
Light	15	28	[6]	[10]	[6]	28
Moderate	-	9	[-]	[-]	[-]	3
Fairly heavy	-	-	[-]	[-]	[-]	-
Heavy	-	3	[-]	[-]	[-]	1
Very heavy	1	-	[-]	[-]	[-]	0
(Fairly heavy + Heavy + Very heavy)	1	3	[-]	[-]	[-]	[-]
Base	50	49	15	22	24	165
Men						
Abstainer***	27	13	16	18	26	20
Occasional drinker	22	24	20	24	14	21
(Abstainer + Occasional)	49	37	36	42	40	42
Light	31	41	43	41	33	37
Moderate	2	12	6	13	16	9
Fairly heavy	9	6	5	[-]	10	7
Heavy	4	3	2	[-]	-	2
Very heavy	6	-	7	4	1	4
(Fairly heavy + Heavy + Very heavy)	18	9	14	4	11	13
Base	165	93	81	40	36	423
All adults						
Abstainer***	32	16	18	19	31	24
Occasional drinker	25	30	22	27	23	25
(Abstainer + Occasional)	57	45	40	46	54	49
Light	27	36	42	43	30	34
Moderate	1	11	6	8	10	7
Fairly heavy	7	4	4	-	6	5
Heavy	3	3	2	-	-	2
Very heavy	5	-	6	2	1	3
(Fairly heavy + Heavy + Very heavy)	14	7	12	2	6	10
Base	215	142	96	62	60	588
% of men and women with alcohol dependence	3%	8%	9%	2%	10%	6%

* Data available for subject interviews only

** Includes 14 residents living in another type of residential accommodation

*** Includes informants who had not had an alcoholic drink in the past 12 months

Table 1.20   Alcohol consumption by age

Residents with schizophrenia, delusional or schizoaffective disorders*

Alcohol consumption level	Age					
	16-24	25-34	35-44	45-54	55-64	All ages
	%	%	%	%	%	%
Abstainer**	[7]	15	17	29	32	24
Occasional drinker	[6]	24	27	27	21	25
Light	[10]	42	38	27	32	34
Moderate	-	16	7	4	4	7
Fairly heavy	[0]	2	.3	9	4	5
Heavy	-	-	1	2	6	2
Very heavy	[2]	1	6	2	2	3
Base	*25*	*116*	*147*	*177*	*124*	*588*

*   Data available for subject interviews only

** Includes informants who had not had an alcoholic drink in the past 12 months

Table 1.21   Use of drugs by type of institution

Residents with schizophrenia, delusional and schizoaffective disorders*

Drugs taken	Hospitals clinics and nursing homes	Residential care homes	Group homes	Hostels	Ordinary housing/ Recognised lodging	All**
		Percentage taking each drug				
Cannabis	**6**	**4**	**9**	**2**	**3**	**5**
Stimulants	**1**	**2**	**1**	**-**	**-**	**1**
Amphetamines	1	2	1	-	-	1
Cocaine/ crack	-	-	-	-	-	-
Hallucinogens inc. Ecstasy	**1**	**1**	**-**	**-**	**-**	**1**
Hallucinogens/psychedelics	1	1	-	-	-	1
Ecstasy	-	-	-	-	-	-
Hypnotics	**1**	**3**	**6**	**2**	**2**	**2**
Sleeping tablets	1	3	3	2	2	2
Tranquilisers	1	2	4	-	2	2
Other drugs	**1**	**-**	**-**	**-**	**-**	**0**
Any drug	**6**	**8**	**13**	**4**	**3**	**7**
Base	*215*	*142*	*96*	*62*	*60*	*588*

*   Data available for subject-interviews only

** Includes 14 residents living in another type of residential accommodation

Table 1.22 Cigarette smoking by sex and type of institution

Residents with schizophrenia, delusional or schizoaffective disorders*

Cigarette smoking	Hospitals clinics and nursing homes	Residential care homes	Group homes	Hostels	Ordinary housing/ Recognised lodging	All**
	%	%	%	%	%	%
Women						
Never regular	38	28	[5]	[7]	[4]	29
Ex- regular	3	5	[1]	[4]	[5]	9
Light	6	11	[1]	[-]	[-]	6
Moderate	24	21	[1]	[2]	[1]	17
Heavy	29	35	[7]	[9]	[12]	39
Base	*50*	*49*	*15*	*22*	*24*	*165*
Men						
Never regular	8	13	11	30	16	12
Ex- regular	5	10	14	6	6	9
Light	7	6	2	-	8	5
Moderate	19	15	19	12	25	18
Heavy	61	56	54	52	46	55
Base	*165*	*93*	*81*	*40*	*36*	*423*
All adults						
Never regular	15	18	14	30	17	17
Ex- regular	5	8	13	11	12	9
Light	6	7	2	-	5	5
Moderate	20	17	17	11	18	18
Heavy	54	49	53	48	49	51
Base	*215*	*142*	*96*	*62*	*60*	*588*

*   Data available for subject interviews only

**   Includes 14 residents living in another type of residential accommodation

Table 1.23 Cigarette smoking behaviours by type of institution

Residents with schizophrenia, delusional or schizoaffective disorders who currently smoked*

	Hospitals clinics and nursing homes	Residential care homes	Group homes	Hostels	Ordinary housing/ Recognised lodging	All**
	%	%	%	%	%	%
How easy not to smoke for a whole day						
Very difficult	63	62	62	81	61	64
Fairly difficult	20	11	28	10	20	18
Fairly easy	9	14	5	8	6	10
Very easy	6	8	5	-	11	7
Don't know	2	4	-	-	3	2
How soon after waking have first cigarette						
Less than 5 minutes	26	33	30	31	32	29
5-14 minutes	32	21	31	22	35	29
15-29 minutes	14	18	16	8	13	14
30 minutes - less than 1 hour	13	18	14	30	12	16
1 hour or more	15	10	9	9	8	12
Whether would like to give up smoking						
Yes	48	55	64	46	57	52
No	47	39	31	42	33	42
Don't know	5	6	5	12	10	6
Base	*168*	*102*	*68*	*37*	*43*	*428*

* Data available for subject interviews only

** Includes 14 residents living in another type of residential accommodation

Table 1.24 Alcohol consumption of cigarette smokers compared with non smokers

Residents with schizophrenia, delusional or schizoaffective disorders*

	Mean units of alcohol consumed per week	Median units of alcohol consumed per week	*Base*
Smokers	8.2	1.1	*440*
Non-Smokers	3.7	0.1	*148*
All	7.0	0.8	*588*

* data available for subject interviews only

2 Residents with affective psychoses

2.1 Introduction

This chapter presents information on economic activity, difficulties with activities of daily living, social functioning and use of alcohol, drugs and tobacco for residents with affective psychoses. Details on the measures used in the analyses in this chapter are found in the *Focus of the report*.

Residents were classified as having affective psychoses if they or staff, acting as proxy informants with the informed consent of the resident, said they were suffering from mania or bipolar affective disorder. Residents were more likely to use expressions such as manic depression or mood swings.

Ninety six residents, approximately 8% of the total institutional sample were identified as having one of these disorders. Because of this relatively small number, analysis by institutional type has been limited to examining differences between residents living in hospitals with those in all types of residential accommodation.

Sixty six per cent of residents with affective psychosis were interviewed themselves; for 29%, responses were obtained from a proxy informant and for the remaining 4% information was obtained from both the subject and a proxy informant. Proxy interviews were obtained for 48% of adults in hospitals, compared with 8% of those in other forms of residential accommodation.

2.2 Descriptive profile of residents

This section shows some of the background characteristics of the group considered in the Chapter. This summarises more detailed information presented in Report 5[1]

Just over half (53%) of residents with affective psychoses were in hospitals, 22% were in residential care homes, 15% were in group homes, 6% were in ordinary housing or recognised lodgings and 4% were in hostels.

Fifty six per cent of residents with affective psychoses were men, 65% were single, and 58% had no qualifications. A quarter of those in this group were divorced, double the proportion of those with schizophrenia. Hospital patients with affective psychoses tended to be younger and less well qualified than those living in residential facilities. *(Table 2.1)*

In all types of institution, the residents' mean length of stay was 4 years yet the median value was two and a half years. This difference was mainly due to the 20% of residents who had been in hospital for at least 10 years. *(Table 2.2)*

Residents with affective psychoses were similar to those with schizophrenia in that just over 70% answered the CIS-R[2] and about 50% of these were ascribed a neurotic disorder. Again, Generalised Anxiety Disorder was found to be the most prevalent disorder, affecting about a third of those with affective psychosis. *(Table 2.3)*

2.3 Economic functioning of residents

Over half the residents with affective psychoses were permanently unable to work (55%); the proportion ranged from 65% of those in hospitals to 44% of those in residential accommodation. Only 18% of those in residential accommodation were working, although 11% were looking for work and 12% were intending to look, but temporarily sick. *(Table 2.4)*

The proportions of those with affective psychoses who controlled their own finances varied significantly by type of institution. Among those in hospitals only 37% did so, with 43% having their finances controlled by an appointee. Among those in residential accommodation three quarters of residents with affective psychosis controlled their own finances. *(Table 2.5)*

Residents who did not live in hospitals, and who controlled their own finances were asked about social security benefits and additional income they received. Almost all were receiving some form of social security benefits (97%); two thirds received Income Support, 44% Invalidity pension and 23% Disability Living Allowance. Income in addition to benefits was received by 36% of those with affective psychoses, generally this was earned income. *(Table 2.6)*

2.4 Activities of daily living (ADL)

All respondents, *except those resident in hospitals*, were asked whether they had any difficulty with regard to 7 activities of daily living. Over half (54%) of residents with affective psychoses had some ADL difficulty. Paperwork was most likely to be difficult (49%); use of transport proved problematic for fewest residents (7%).

There were no residents who reported needing help with an ADL and who did not receive such help. Due to the small proportions who did in fact need assistance, it was not possible to analyse who provided the help. *(Tables 2.7, 2.8 and 2.9)*

2.5 Social functioning of residents

Perceived social support

Only a quarter of residents with affective psychoses perceived no lack of social support; 42% perceived a severe lack of social support and a further 30% had a moderate lack. *(Table 2.10)*

Extent of social networks

In this survey information about social networks focused on the numbers of friends, including staff, and relatives (aged 16 and over) respondents felt close to.

Only 4% of residents with affective psychoses had no close friends or relatives. However, within their place of residence, 39% felt close to no other person and 3% lived alone. Although 36% had no close friends outside of the establishment, 85% said they had close relatives. A total primary support group of 3 or fewer was found for only 18% of residents with affective psychoses, putting this group in a better position than other residents in institutions. *(Tables 2.11 and 2.12)*

Leisure activities

Residents with affective psychoses in hospitals participated in a mean of 6 leisure activities while those in residential accommodation had a slightly higher mean, 7. Among the hospital residents, 24% pursued only 3 or fewer leisure activities, compared with only 8% of those in residential accommodation. *(Table 2.13)*

Regardless of type of institution, watching TV and listening to music were the most popular activities. While 57% of residents with affective psychoses read books and newspapers and 32% participated in sports, the corresponding proportions for those in hospitals were 38% and 17%. *(Table 2.14)*

2.6 Use of alcohol, drugs and tobacco

This section looks at alcohol use, drug misuse, and cigarette smoking among residents with affective psychoses.

Drug misuse includes the use of illegal drugs such as cannabis, stimulants and hallucinogens, and the extra-medical use of prescription medicines. The consumption of prescribed medication in general was covered in Report 5 of this series of reports on psychiatric morbidity[3].

Alcohol consumption

The methodology used on this survey to categorise alcohol consumption and alcohol dependence is described in the *focus of this report*.

Over half (56%) of those with affective psychoses were non-, or occasional drinkers, while 10% drank more than the recommended sensible level. Heavy drinking was more prevalent in hospitals than in residential accommodation, and particularly among men compared with women. Alcohol dependence was reported for 8%. *(Tables 2.16 and 2.17)*

Drug use

Eighteen per cent of residents with affective psychoses were defined as drug users, with the proportion considerably higher among those in residential accommodation, compared with those in hospitals. Ten per cent had taken hypnotics to get high, or more than their prescribed dose (8% tranquillisers and 6% sleeping tablets); 8% used cannabis and 4% used hallucinogens. *(Table 2.18)*

Cigarette smoking

Half the residents with affective psychoses were heavy cigarette smokers, only a quarter did not regularly smoke. Sixty three per cent of those who currently smoked said that they would find it very difficult not to smoke for a whole day, however 58% reported that they would like to give up. *(Tables 2.19 and 2.20)*

Notes and references

1. Meltzer, H., Gill, B., Hinds, K., and Petticrew, M., (1996) *OPCS Surveys of Psychiatric Morbidity in Great Britain, Report 5: Physical complaints, service use and treatment of residents with psychiatric disorders*. HMSO: London

2. Lewis, G., Pelosi, A.J., and Dunn, G.,(1992) Measuring Psychiatric disorder in the community; a standardised assessment for use by interviewers, *Psychological Medicine,* **22**, 465–486

   Lewis, G., and Pelosi, A.J., *Manual of the Revised Clinical Interview Schedule (CIS–R)*, June 1990, MRC Institute of Psychiatry

3. Meltzer, H., Gill, B., Hinds, K., and Petticrew, M., (1996) *OPCS Surveys of Psychiatric Morbidity in Great Britain, Report 5: Physical complaints, service use and treatment of residents with psychiatric disorders*. HMSO: London

Table 2.1 Personal characteristics of residents by type of institution

Residents with affective psychoses

	Hospitals clinics & nursing homes	All forms of residential accommodation	All
	%	%	%
Sex			
Men	60	56	58
Women	40	44	42
Age			
16-34	49	23	37
35-44	11	31	20
45-54	25	26	26
55-64	15	20	17
Marital status			
Married/cohabiting	3	6	4
Single	72	57	65
Widowed	1	4	2
Divorced	22	26	24
Separated	2	7	4
Ethnicity			
White or European	92	95	94
West Indian or African	2	-	1
Asian or Oriental	1	5	3
Other	5	-	3
Qualifications			
A levels or higher	12	9	11
GCSE/O level	16	40	27
Other qualifications	7	2	4
No qualifications	64	50	58
Base	*51*	*45*	*96*

Table 2.2 Residence charateristics of residents by type of institution

Residents with affective psychoses

	Hospitals clinics and nursing homes	All forms of residential accommodation	All
	%	%	%
Length of stay			
ess than 1 year	35	30	32
1 year < 2 years	18	7	13
2 years < 3 years	10	24	17
3 years < 4 years	3	7	5
4 years < 5 years	7	4	6
5 years < 6 years	-	6	3
6 years < 7 years	1	15	7
7 years < 8 years	1	3	2
8 years < 9 years	3	2	2
9 years < 10 years	2	-	1
10 years < 15 years	12	1	6
15 years < 20 years	3	-	1
20 years < 25 years	5	-	2
Mean length of stay			
(years)	**4.7**	**3.1**	**4.0**
(Mean age)	**(38)**	**(43)**	**(41)**
Median length of stay			
(years)	**1.5**	**2.5**	**2.5**
(Median age)	**(35)**	**(42)**	**(38)**
Where subject was living			
before present institution			
	%	%	%
Hospital, clinic or nursing home	36	45	40
Private household	47	24	36
Supported accommodation/ group home	3	15	8
Residential care home	7	10	8
Prison/ on remand	5	-	3
B&B/ Hotel/ Hostel	1	6	4
Other	1	-	1
Base	*51*	*45*	*96*

Table 2.3 Neurotic disorders and significant neurotic symptoms (as measured by the CIS-R)

Residents with affective psychoses who answered the CIS-R

	%
Number of neurotic disorders	
0	48
1	22
2	16
3	12
4	1
Any neurotic disorder	**52**

	Percentage affected
Type of neurotic disorder	
Generalised Anxiety Disorder	35
Depressive episode	22
Phobia	12
Obsessive-Compulsive Disorder	12
Mixed anxiety and depressive disorder	9
Panic	5

	Percentage affected
Significant neurotic symptoms	
Fatigue	49
Sleep problems	42
Anxiety	42
Worry	40
Depressive ideas	36
Depression	35
Concentration/forgetfulness	31
Irritability	24
Obsessions	22
Somatic symptoms	22
Worry about physical health	20
Compulsions	15
Phobia	13
Panic	12
Base	*69*

Table 2.4 Economic activity by type of Institution

Residents with affective psychoses

Economic activity	Hospitals clinics and nursing homes	All forms of residential accommodation	All
	%	%	%
Permanently unable to work	65	44	55
Working	14	18	16
Intending to look, temporarily sick	2	12	7
Looking for work	0	11	5
Retired	2	3	3
Full time education	-	3	2
Waiting to take up a job	1	-	1
Other	16	8	12
Base	*51*	*45*	*96*

Table 2.5 Control of financial affairs by type of institution

Residents with affective psychoses

Who controls finances?	Hospitals clinics and nursing homes	All forms of residential accommodation dation	All
	%	%	%
Self	37	75	55
Appointee (eg relative, friend)	43	9	27
Member of staff	14	13	14
DSS direct payments	1	2	2
Court of protection	5	2	4
Base	*51*	*45*	*96*

Table 2.6 Receipt of benefits, and other sources of income among adults controlling their own finances

Residents with affective psychoses*

Social security benefits and other sources of income received	All forms of residential accommodation
	Percentage receiving
Social security benefits	
Income Support	65
Invalidity pension	44
Disability Living Allowance	23
N.I Sickness Benefit	6
Severe Disablement Allowance	4
Other benefits**	8
Receiving any benefits	97
Receiving no benefits	3
Other sources of income	
Earned income	21
Interest from saving	8
Pension from former employer	4
Other regular sources of alimony	3
Any other source	5
Any additional income	36
No additional income	64
Base	*33*

*   Data not available for adults who did not control their own
     finances; residents in hospitals were not asked about Social
     security benefits or other sources of income
** Including Old Age benefits,War Widow's pension and other
     benefits

Table 2.7 Number of ADL difficulties

Residents with affective psychoses*

Number of ADL difficulties	All forms of residential accommodation
	%
0	46
1	24
2	11
3	7
4	10
5+	2
Base	*45*

* These data were not collected for adults in hospitals

Table 2.8 Activities of daily living difficulties

*Residents with affective psychoses**

Type of difficulty	Whether problem	All forms of residential accommodation
		%
Dealing with paperwork	problem	49
	not problem	51
	does not apply	-
Household activities	problem	20
	not problem	78
	does not apply	1
Managing money	problem	18
	not problem	82
	does not apply	-
Medical care	problem	11
	not problem	85
	does not apply	4
Practical activities	problem	10
	not problem	59
	does not apply	31
Personal care	problem	9
	not problem	91
	does not apply	-
Use of transport	problem	7
	not problem	93
	does not apply	-
Difficulty with any of the above		**54**
Base		*45*

* These data were not collected for adults in hospitals

Table 2.9 Need for help by type of ADL difficulty

Residents with affective psychoses

Type of difficulty	All forms of residential accommodation
All adults	%
Dealing with paperwork	
Has difficulty, needs help, gets help	49
Has difficulty, needs help, gets no help	-
Has difficulty, needs no help	-
Has no difficulty	51
Does not apply	-
Managing money	
Has difficulty, needs help, gets help	15
Has difficulty, needs help, gets no help	-
Has difficulty, needs no help	3
Has no difficulty	82
Does not apply	-
Household activities	
Has difficulty, needs help, gets help	20
Has difficulty, needs help, gets no help	-
Has difficulty, needs no help	-
Has no difficulty	78
Does not apply	1
Medical care	
Has difficulty, needs help, gets help	10
Has difficulty, needs help, gets no help	-
Has difficulty, needs no help	1
Has no difficulty	85
Does not apply	4
Use of transport	
Has difficulty, needs help, gets help	4
Has difficulty, needs help, gets no help	-
Has difficulty, needs no help	4
Has no difficulty	93
Does not apply	-
Practical activities	
Has difficulty, needs help, gets help	10
Has difficulty, needs help, gets no help	-
Has difficulty, needs no help	-
Has no difficulty	59
Does not apply	31
Personal care	
Has difficulty, needs help, gets help	5
Has difficulty, needs help, gets no help	-
Has difficulty, needs no help	4
Has no difficulty	91
Does not apply	-
Difficulty with any of the above	**54**
Base	*45*

* These data were not collected for adults in hospitals

Table 2.10 Perceived social support by type of institution

Residents with affective psychoses*

Level of perceived social support	Hospitals clinics and nursing homes	All forms of residential accommodation	All
	%	%	%
No lack	[6]	28	26
Moderate lack	[8]	30	30
Severe lack	[11]	42	42
Unclassified	[2]	-	2
Base	*27*	*41*	*68*

* Data available for subject interviews only

Table 2.11 Extent of social networks by type of institution

Residents with affective psychoses*

Type and size of social network	Hospitals clinics and nursing homes	All forms of residential accommodation	All
	%	%	%
Household members that feel close to**			
0	[13]	34	39
1	[4]	25	20
2	[3]	9	10
3	[2]	12	10
4 or more	[5]	17	18
Live alone	-	4	3
Relatives that don't live with, that feel close to**			
0	[3]	18	15
1	[5] [15]	14 54	16 54
2	[7]	22	24
3	[3]	15	13
4	[1]	6	5
5	[2]	7	7
6	[4]	9	11
7	[1]	-	1
8	[1]	2	2
9	[-]	-	-
10 or more	[2]	7	7
Friends outside of household that feel close to**			
0	[12]	28	36
1	[3] [17]	16 52	14 58
2	[2]	8	8
3	[1]	19	13
4	[2]	11	11
5	[1]	7	6
6	[-]	4	2
7	[-]	-	-
8	[-]	4	2
9	[-]	-	-
10	[2]	3	5
11	[-]	-	-
12	[-]	-	-
13 or more	[2]	-	3
Percentage of adults with no close friends or relatives	[0]	6	4
Base	*27*	*41*	*68*

* Data available for subject interviews only
** Percentages within each group total 100%

Table 2.12 Size of primary support group by type of institution

Residents with affective psychoses*

Size of primary support group	Hospitals clinics and nursing homes	All forms of residential accommodation	All
	%	%	%
9 or more	[7]	24	26
4 - 8	[15]	58	57
0 - 3	[5]	18	18
Base	27	41	68

* Data available for subject interviews only

Table 2.13 Use of leisure time by type of institution

Residents with affective psychoses

Use of leisure time	Hospitals clinics and nursing homes	All forms of residential accommo-dation	All
	%	%	%
Number of activities involved in			
Mean in and around the establishment	2.8	3.2	3.0
Mode in and around the establishment	1.0	2.0	1.0
Mean outside the establishment	3.3	4.2	3.7
Mode outside the establishment	3.0	3.0	3.0
Mean total	6.1	7.3	6.7
Modal total	8.0	5.0	5.0
Percentage involved in			
Total number of activities			
0-3	24	8	16
4-9	63	69	66
10 or more	14	23	18
Base	51	45	96

Table 2.14 Leisure activities by type of institution

Residents with affective psychoses

Leisure activities	Hospitals clinics and nursing homes	All forms of residential accommo-dation	All
	Percentage participating in each activity		
In and around the establishment			
TV/radio	89	86	88
Listening to music	73	78	76
Entertaining friends or relatives	40	56	48
Reading books and newspapers	38	57	47
Writing letters/ telephoning	55	35	46
Games	29	28	28
Hobbies	25	25	25
Gardening	6	18	12
DIY/ car maintenance	0	4	2
Any activity	99	98	98
No activity	1	2	2
Out of the establishment			
Shopping	68	68	68
Going for a walk, walking the dog	66	60	63
Visiting friends or relatives	57	64	60
Pubs, restaurants	42	52	47
Sports as a participant	17	32	24
Cinema, theatre, concerts	19	22	20
Library	3	36	19
Church	16	16	16
Sports as a spectator	13	12	12
Clubs, organisations	4	11	8
Classes, lectures	2	13	7
Bingo, amusement arcades	5	8	6
Bookmakers, betting and gambling	5	6	6
Night clubs, discos	2	6	4
Political activities	-	3	1
Any activity	91	95	93
No activity	9	5	7
Base	51	45	96

Table 2.15 Attendance at social, training, or educational centres by type of institution

Residents with affective psychoses

	Hospitals clinics and nursing homes	Residential homes	All
	Percentage attending each type of centre		
Day centre	5	36	20
Club for people with mental health problems	6	30	17
Club for people with physical health problems	-	-	-
Other social club	19	12	16
Adult education centre	2	7	4
Adult training centre	-	-	-
Base	50	46	96

Table 2.16 Alcohol consumption and dependence by type of institution

*Residents with affective psychoses**

Alcohol consumption level	Hospitals clinics and nursing homes		All forms of residential accommodation		All	
	%		%		%	
Abstainer**	[10]		16		24	
Occasional drinker	[9]	[19]	31	48	32	56
Light	[1]		37		24	
Moderate	[2]		10		10	
Fairly heavy	[1]		1		2	
Heavy	[1]	[4]	2	5	3	10
Very heavy	[2]		2		5	
Base	27		41		68	
Percentage with alcohol dependence	**16%**		**3%**		**8%**	

* Data available for subject interviews only
** Includes informants who had not had an alcoholic drink in the past 12 months

Table 2.17 Alcohol consumption by sex

*Residents with affective psychoses**

Alcohol consumption level	Women		Men		All	
	%		%		%	
Abstainer**	[11]		13		24	
Occasional drinker	[11]	[22]	25	38	32	56
Light	[2]		34		24	
Moderate	[-]		16		10	
Fairly heavy	[1]		1		2	
Heavy	[-]	[2]	5	12	3	10
Very heavy	[1]		6		5	
Base	27		40		68	

* Data available for subject interviews only
** Includes informants who had not had an alcoholic drink in the past 12 months

Table 2.18 Use of drugs by type of institution

*Residents with affective psychoses**

Drugs taken	Hospitals clinics and nursing homes	All forms of residential accommodation	All
	Percentage taking each drug		
Cannabis	**6**	**10**	**8**
Stimulants	**0**	**4**	**2**
Amphetamines	0	4	2
Cocaine/crack	-	-	-
Hallucinogens inc Ecstasy	**4**	**4**	**4**
Hallucinogens/psychedelics	4	0	2
Ecstasy	0	4	2
Hypnotics	**1**	**15**	**10**
Sleeping tablets	1	10	6
Tranquilisers	1	12	8
Other drugs	**-**	**-**	**-**
Solvents	-	-	-
Opiates	-	-	-
Heroin	-	-	-
Any drug	**7**	**25**	**18**
Base	27	41	68

* Data available for subject interviews only

Table 2.19 Cigarette smoking by type of institution

*Residents with affective psychoses**

Cigarette smoking	Hospitals clinics and nursing homes	All forms of residential accommodation	All
	%	%	%
Never regular	[7]	26	26
Ex-regular	[0]	7	5
Light	[1]	9	7
Moderate	[6]	7	14
Heavy	[12]	51	49
Base	*27*	*41*	*68*

* Data available for subject interviews only

Table 2.20 Cigarette smoking behaviours

*Residents with affective psychoses who currently smoked**

	All
	%
How easy not to smoke for a whole day	
Very difficult	63
Fairly difficult	19
Fairly easy	9
Very easy	10
Don't know	-
How soon after waking have first cigarette	
Less than 5 minutes	34
5-14 minutes	17
15-29 minutes	10
30 minutes - less than 1 hour	24
1 hour or more	14
Whether would like to give up smoking	
Yes	58
No	37
Don't know	4
Base	*47*

* Data available for subject interviews only

Table 2.21 Alcohol consumption of cigarette smokers compared with non–smokers

*Residents with affective psychoses**

	Mean units of alcohol per week	Median units of alcohol per week	*Base*
Smokers	8.7	0.4	*47*
Non-Smokers	[5.3]	[0.3]	*21*
All	7.7	0.3	*68*

* Data available for subject interviews only

3 Residents with neurotic disorders

3.1 Introduction

This chapter presents information on economic activity, difficulties with activities of daily living, social functioning and the use of alcohol, drugs and tobacco for residents with neurotic disorders. Details of the measures used in the analysis are given in the *focus of the report*.

Residents with neurotic disorders represented 8% of those living in institutions catering specifically for people with mental health problems. Over three quarters of them were living in some type of residential accommodation. This group of residents, like all others in the survey, were asked to say what was the matter with them. Because they did not say anything indicative of schizophrenia or affective psychosis, their ascribed diagnosis was based on the CIS-R interview[1]. As the CIS-R interview was not conducted by proxy, all residents categorised as having a neurotic disorder were interviewed in person.

Some of the types of accommodation in which this group were living could have been picked up on the private household survey. For example, 80% of those in group homes or ordinary housing/recognised lodging would have been eligible for a survey of people living in private households. However, it is important to note that residents of institutions with neurotic disorders were more similar to residents of institutions with other disorders, than to those identified on the private household survey as having neurotic disorders. Firstly, a third of these residents, mostly living in group homes and ordinary housing/ recognised lodgings, reported taking antipsychotic drugs. This suggests that this particular group of residents, had previously had a psychotic illness, but no longer considered themselves to have this illness. Many were likely to be in the process of reintegrating themselves into the community. Among adults identified as having neurotic disorders on the private household survey no-one reported taking antipsychotic drugs[2]. Further differences are highlighted in the following section.

3.2 Descriptive profile of residents

This section presents some basic characteristics of the individuals and institutions covered in this chapter. More detailed information is found in Report 5[3]. Some comparisons with adults with neurotic disorders identified in the Private Household Survey are also made.

A third of residents with neurotic disorders were living in residential care homes (32%), 23% were in hostels, 20% were in hospitals and 18% were in group homes. The remaining 7% lived in ordinary housing or recognised lodging. Due to the broad spread between the types of accommodation, and the small number of adults overall (101), data in this chapter are not analysed by type of institution.

As with other residents of institutions, those with neurotic disorders were predominantly male (61%) and middle-aged. Their mean age was 40 and about two-thirds had never been married. In the private household survey, the majority of adults identified as having neurotic disorders were female (62%) and most were married or cohabiting (61%). Compared with residents with other disorders, those with neurotic disorders tended to be slightly better qualified with half of them having some educational qualifications and 1 in 5 having reached at least A level standard. (*Table 3.1*)

The most marked difference between residents with neurotic disorders and those with other psychiatric complaints was that the mean length of stay in their present accommodation of the neurotic group was far shorter, 2.2 years (compared with 5.3 years for those with schizophrenia). Nearly a half of all residents with neurotic disorders had entered their present accommodation from private households, but most had previously been in other forms of institutionalised accommodation. (*Table 3.2*)

Half of all residents with neurotic disorders said they had a longstanding physical complaint (this is identical to the proportion among adults with neurosis identified on the private household survey).

Compared with adults identified on the private household survey as having neurotic disorders, the proportions of residents with neurotic disorders having mixed anxiety and depression, Generalised Anxiety Disorder and Panic disorder were almost identical. However, the proportions having phobia and Obsessive-Compulsive Disorder were almost double among the group in institutions. Depressive episode was recorded for 20% of institutional residents with neurotic disorders compared with 14% of those identified as having a neurotic disorder on the private household survey. Residents with neurosis were more likely to have comorbid neurotic disorders; 68% had just one disorder compared with 87% of those in the private household survey.

Regarding neurotic symptoms identified on the CIS-R, those with neurotic disorders in institutions were more likely than those in the private household survey to have depression, depressive ideas, anxiety and phobia, and notably less likely to have fatigue and irritability.(*Table 3.3*)

3.3 Economic functioning of residents

Just over half of residents with neurotic

disorders were permanently unable to work (52%). Thirteen per cent were intending to look for work, but were temporarily sick; the same proportion as were actually working. Six per cent had jobs, but had been away from them in the last week. Among adults with neurotic disorders identified in the private household survey, 9% of women and 16% of men were classified as permanently unable to work. (*Table 3.4*)

Almost two thirds (63%) of those with neurotic disorders controlled their own finances. For one in five, an appointee, such as a friend or relative, took control and for one in 10, a member of staff did. (*Table 3.5*)

Residents who did not live in hospitals, and who controlled their own finances were asked about social security benefits and additional income they may receive. Seventy-one per cent were receiving some form of social security benefits; 35% received Income Support, 30% Invalidity benefit and 15% Disability living allowance. Income in addition to benefits was received by 31% of those with neurotic disorders, generally this was earned by the respondent (22%); 10% were receiving interest from savings and investment. (*Table 3.6*)

3.4 Activities of daily living (ADL)

Two thirds of residents with neurotic disorders had some ADL difficulty. Almost a half reported difficulty with paperwork and a quarter had problems with each of managing money and using transport. Personal care was least likely to be a problem, proving difficult for only 5%.

Most adults who reported needing help with an ADL received help. No more than 2% of residents reported needing help which they did not receive for any ADL difficulty. Due to the small proportions who did in fact need assistance, it was not possible to analyse who provided the help. (*Tables 3.7, 3.8, 3.9*)

3.5 Social functioning of residents

Perceived social support

Forty four per cent of residents with neurotic disorders perceived a severe lack of social support and a further 20% had a moderate lack. The level could not be determined for 7%. It is interesting that the proportion of residents with neurotic disorders who felt a severe lack of social support was identical to that found among residents with schizophrenia (43%). This is notably higher than among adults with neurotic disorders identified in the private household survey, 17% of whom reported a severe lack of social support. (*Table 3.10*)

Extent of social networks

Almost all of the residents with neurotic disorders had at least one close friend or relative. However, within their place of residence, 39% did not feel close to other residents and 3% lived alone. Almost two thirds (64%) had no more than 2 close friends outside of their establishments. Total primary support groups of 3 or fewer were found among 30% of residents with neurotic disorders and only 18% had 9 or more people in their primary support group. (*Tables 3.11 and 3.12*)

Leisure activities

All residents were asked about their participation in 26 specific leisure and social activities, both in and out of the establishment.

Residents with neurotic disorders participated in a mean of 3 leisure activities in and around the establishment, and 4 outside of it. While the mean total was 6, the modal total was 2 showing that a few people who were very active in their leisure time considerably inflated the mean. One in five residents pursued 10 or more leisure activities while a third were involved in 3 or fewer such activities.

By far the most popular activity was watching the TV (85%), followed by listening to the radio (70%). Just over half (58%) of residents with neurotic disorders visited friends or relatives, although only 21% entertained friends or relatives. Under a quarter (23%) of residents with neurotic disorders participated in sport.(*Tables 3.13 , 3.14 and 3.15*)

3.6 Use of alcohol, drugs and tobacco

Alcohol consumption

Forty per cent of those with neurotic disorders were non-, or occasional drinkers, while 14% drank more than the recommended sensible level. The proportion of non-drinkers or those who drank occasionally increased from 29% among 16-39 year olds to 47% among those aged 40-64 . Men were more likely to be heavy drinkers than were women (16% compared with 10%). Alcohol dependence was reported for 7%. (*Tables 3.16 and 3.17*)

Drug use

Just under a quarter (22%) of residents with neurotic disorders had used some drug; 11% had taken cannabis, 8% tranquillisers and 6% sleeping tablets. Other drugs had been taken by 2% or fewer. (*Table 3.18*)

Cigarette smoking

Three quarters of residents with neurotic disorders were light, moderate or heavy cigarette smokers; the majority in fact smoked heavily (46% of men and 24% of women). (*Table 3.19*)

Sixty nine per cent of those who smoked regularly said they would find it very difficult not to smoke for a whole day. Almost half (45%) reported usually having their first cigarette of the day within 5 minutes of waking. Over half of those who smoked regularly did not want to give up; 41% said they would like to stop smoking. (*Table 3.20*)

Notes and references

1. Lewis, G., Pelosi, A.J., and Dunn, G.,(1992) Measuring Psychiatric disorder in the community: a standardised assessment for use by interviewers, *Psychological Medicine*, **22**, 465–486

    Lewis, G., and Pelosi, A.J., *Manual of the Revised Clinical Interview Schedule (CIS–R)*, June 1990, MRC Institute of Psychiatry

2. Meltzer, H., Gill, B., Petticrew, M., and Hinds, K., (1995) *OPCS Surveys of Psychiatric Morbidity in Great Britain, Report 2: Physical complaints, service use and treatment of adults with psychiatric disorders*. HMSO: London

3. Meltzer, H., Gill, B., Hinds, K., and Petticrew, M., (1996) *OPCS Surveys of Psychiatric Morbidity in Great Britain, Report 5: Physical complaints, service use and treatment of residents with psychiatric disorders*. HMSO: London

Table 3.1   Personal characteristics of residents by sex

Residents with neurotic disorders

	Men	Women	All
	%	%	%
Age			
16-24	14	33	21
25-34	16	21	18
35-44	22	20	21
45-54	23	14	20
55-64	26	12	20
Marital status			
Married/cohabiting	9	17	12
Single	66	64	65
Widowed	2	-	1
Divorced	18	19	19
Separated	5	-	3
Ethnicity			
White or European	96	89	93
West Indian or African	4	-	2
Asian or Oriental	1	7	3
Other	-	4	2
Qualifications			
A levels or higher	12	27	18
GCSE/O levels	24	6	17
Other qualifications	14	13	14
No qualifications	50	54	51
Base	*62*	*39*	*101*
% of men and women with neurotic disorders	61%	39%	100%

Table 3.2   Residence characteristics of residents

Residents with neurotic disorders

	%
Length of stay	
Less than 1 year	39
1 year < 2 years	18
2 years < 3 years	16
3 years < 4 years	11
4 years < 5 years	5
5 years < 6 years	6
6 years < 7 years	3
7 years < 8 years	-
8 years < 9 years	2
9 years < 10 years	-
10 years < 15 years	1
Mean length of stay (years)	**2.2**
(Mean age)	**(40)**
Median length of stay (years)	**1.5**
Median age)	**(40)**
Where subject was living	
before present institution	
Private household	46
Hospital, clinic or nursing home	21
Residential care home	13
B&B/ Hotel/ Hostel	10
Supported accommodation/ group home	7
Prison/ on remand	2
Base	*101*

Table 3.3 Neurotic disorders and significant neurotic symptoms (as measured by the CIS-R); residents with neurotic disorders compared with adults identified as having neurotic disorders in the private household survey

	Resident with neurotic disorders who answered the CIS-R	Adults identified as having a neurotic disorder in the private household survey
	%	%
Number of neurotic disorders		
1	68	87
2	19	9
3	9	3
4	3	1

Percentage of adults with each neurotic disorder

Type of neurotic disorder		
Generalised Anxiety Disorder	47	48
Mixed anxiety and depressive disorder	27	28
Phobia	26	12
Depressive episode	20	14
Obsessive-Compulsive Disorder	19	10
Panic	7	6

Percentage of adults with each neurotic sympton

Significant neurotic symptoms		
Depressive ideas	68	46
Worry	63	67
Sleep problems	59	63
Anxiety	59	47
Fatigue	56	77
Depression	56	43
Irritability	46	61
Obsessions	43	35
Concentration/forgetfulness	42	36
Phobia	39	22
Worry about physical health	34	19
Compulsions	29	20
Somatic symptoms	28	29
Panic	23	15
Base	*101*	*1557*

Table 3.4 Economic activity

Residents with neurotic disorders

Economic activity	
	%
Permanently unable to work	52
Working	13
Intending to look, temporarily sick	13
Has job, but away last week	6
Retired	6
Looking for work	4
Keeping house	1
Other	5
Base	*101*

Table 3.5 Control of finances

Residents with neurotic disorders

Who controls finances*

	Percentage with finances controlled by:
Self	63
Appointee (eg relative, friend)	21
Member of staff	11
DSS direct payments	4
Bank	1
Court of protection	0
Base	*101*

* Adults who did not control their own financial affairs could have more than one alternative source of control

Table 3.6 Receipt of benefits and other sources of income

Residents with neurotic disorders who controlled their own finances*

Social security benefits and other sources of income received

	Percentage receiving
Social security benefits	
Income Support	40
Invalidity pension	34
Disability Living Allowance	18
N.I sickness benefit	2
Severe Disablement Allowance	4
Other benefits**	20
Receiving any benefits	**81**
Receiving no benefits	**19**
Other sources of income	
Earned income	25
Interest from savings, investments etc	12
Pension from former employer	2
Any other source	4
Any additional income	**36**
No additional income	**64**
Base	*56*

* data not available for adults who did not control their own finances; residents in hospitals were not asked about social security benefits or other sources of income

** including old age benefits, war widows pension and other benefits

Table 3.7 Number of ADL difficulties

Residents with neurotic disorders*

Number of ADL difficulties	%
0	33
1	24
2	32
3	2
4	6
5 or more	4
Base	*82*

* These data were not collected for adults in hospitals

Table 3.8 Activities of daily living difficulties

Residents with neurotic disorders

Type of difficulty	Whether problem	
		%
Dealing with paperwork	problem	45
	not problem	54
	does not apply	1
Managing money	problem	25
	not problem	70
	does not apply	5
Use of transport	problem	24
	not problem	76
	does not apply	-
Household activities	problem	15
	not problem	81
	does not apply	4
Medical care	problem	12
	not problem	86
	does not apply	2
Practical activities	problem	8
	not problem	57
	does not apply	34
Personal care	problem	5
	not problem	95
	does not apply	-
Difficulty with any of the above		**67**
Base		*82*

* These data were not collected for adults in hospitals

Table 3.9   Need for help by type of ADL difficulty

Residents with neurotic disorders

Type of difficulty	%
Dealing with paperwork	
Has difficulty, needs help, gets help	44
Has difficulty, needs help, gets no help	-
Has difficulty, needs no help	1
Has no difficulty	54
Does not apply	1
Managing money	
Has difficulty, needs help, gets help	20
Has difficulty, needs help, gets no help	2
Has difficulty, needs no help	3
Has no difficulty	70
Does not apply	5
Household activities	
Has difficulty, needs help, gets help	11
Has difficulty, needs help, gets no help	2
Has difficulty, needs no help	2
Has no difficulty	81
Does not apply	4
Medical care	
Has difficulty, needs help, gets help	9
Has difficulty, needs help, gets no help	-
Has difficulty, needs no help	1
Has no difficulty	88
Does not apply	2
Use of transport	
Has difficulty, needs help, gets help	13
Has difficulty, needs help, gets no help	2
Has difficulty, needs no help	9
Has no difficulty	76
Does not apply	-
Practical activities	
Has difficulty, needs help, gets help	6
Has difficulty, needs help, gets no help	2
Has difficulty, needs no help	-
Has no difficulty	57
Does not apply	34
Personal care	
Has difficulty, needs help, gets help	4
Has difficulty, needs help, gets no help	-
Has difficulty, needs no help	1
Has no difficulty	95
Does not apply	-
Difficulty with any of the above	**67**
Base	*82*

Table 3.10   Perceived social support

*Residents with neurotic disorders**

Level of perceived social support	%
No lack	30
Moderate lack	20
Severe lack	44
Unclassified	6
Base	*99*

* data available for subject interviews only

Table 3.11   Extent of social networks

Residents with neurotic disorders*

Type and size of social network	%
Household members that feel close to:**	
0	39
1	16
2	21
3	8
4 or more	12
Live alone	3
Relatives that don't live with, that feel close to: **	
0	26
1	27
2	18
3	8
4	3
5	6
6	4
7	3
8	2
9	-
10 or more	4

(0–2: 70)

Friends outside of household that feel close to: **	
0	34
1	16
2	15
3	12
4	8
5	5
6	6
7	-
8	-
9	-
10	2
11	-
12	-
13 or more	3

(0–2: 64)

Percentage of adults with no close friends or relatives	2
Base	*99*

*   data available for subject interviews only

** Percentages within each group total 100%

Table 3.12   Size of primary support group

Residents with neurotic disorders*

Size of primary support group	%
9 or more	18
4 - 8	52
0 - 3	30
Base	*99*

* Data available for subject interviews only

Table 3.13   Use of leisure time

Residents with neurotic disorders

Use of leisure time	
Number of activities involved in	
Mean in and around the establishment	2.6
Mode in and around the establishment	1.0
Mean outside the establishment	3.6
Mode outside the establishment	2.0
Mean total	6.2
Modal total	2.0
Total number of activities	**%**
0 - 3	34
4 - 9	46
10 or more	20
Base	*101*

Table 3.14   Leisure activities

Residents with neurotic disorders

Leisure activities

	Percentage participating in each activity:
In and around establishment	
TV/ radio	85
Listening to music	70
Reading books and newspapers	45
Hobbies	36
Writing letters/ telephoning	32
Games	31
Entertaining friends or relatives	21
Gardening	9
DIY/ car maintenance	8
Any activity	98
No activity	2
Out of the establishment	
Visiting friends or relatives	58
Shopping	53
Pubs, restaurants	45
Going for a walk, walking the dog	44
Cinema, theatre, concerts	28
Library	27
Sports as a participant	23
Night clubs, discos	18
Clubs, organisations	17
Church	12
Classes, lectures	10
Bingo, amusement arcades	8
Bookmakers, betting and gambling	4
Sports as a spectator	4
Political activities	-
Any activity	85
No activity	15
Base	*101*

Table 3.15   Attendance at social, training, or educational centres

Residents with neurotic disorders

	Percentage attending each type of centre
Day centre	19
Club for people with mental health problems	11
Club for people with physical health problems	1
Other social club	10
Adult education centre	3
Adult training centre	2
Base	*101*

Table 3.16   Alcohol consumption by age

Residents with neurotic disorders*

Alcohol consumption level	Age		
	16 - 39	40 - 64	All
	%	%	%
Abstainer**	10 ⎤ 29	32 ⎤ 47	23 ⎤ 40
Occasional drinker	18 ⎦	16 ⎦	17 ⎦
Light	32	30	31
Moderate	23	10	16
Fairly heavy	9 ⎤	7 ⎤	8 ⎤
Heavy	3 ⎥ 17	2 ⎥ 12	3 ⎥ 14
Very heavy	5 ⎦	2 ⎦	3 ⎦
Base	*39*	*60*	*99*

*   Data available for subject interviews only

** Includes informants who had not had an alcoholic drink in the
     past 12 months

43

Table 3.17 Alcohol consumption by sex

Residents with neurotic disorders*

Alcohol consumption level	Women	Men	All
	%	%	%
Abstainer**	24	23	23
Occasional drinker	28 (51)	10 (33)	17 (40)
Light	21	37	31
Moderate	18	14	16
Fairly heavy	9	7	8
Heavy	1 (10)	4 (16)	3 (14)
Very heavy	-	6	3
Base	39	60	99

* Data available for subject interviews only

** Includes informants who had not had an alcoholic drink in the past 12 months

Table 3.18 Use of drugs

Residents with neurotic disorders*

Drugs taken	Percentage taking each drug:
Cannabis	**11**
Stimulants	**2**
Amphetamines	2
Cocaine/ crack	-
Hallucinogens inc. Ecstasy	**1**
Hallucinogens/ psychedelics	1
Ecstasy	0
Hypnotics	**12**
Sleeping tablets	6
Tranquilisers	8
Other drugs	**2**
Solvents	1
Opiates	0
Heroin	1
Any drug	**22**
Base	99

* Data available for subject interviews only

Table 3.19 Cigarette smoking by sex

Residents with neurotic disorders*

Cigarette smoking	Women	Men	All
	%	%	%
Never regular	20	6	11
Ex- regular	6	21	15
Light	10	8	9
Moderate	30	20	24
Heavy	34	46	41
Base	39	60	99

* Data available for subject interviews only

Table 3.20 Cigarette smoking behaviours

Residents with neurotic disorders who currently smoked*

	%
How easy not to smoke for a whole day	
Very difficult	69
Fairly difficult	8
Fairly easy	14
Very easy	9
Don't know	-
How soon after waking have first cigarette	
Less than 5 minutes	45
5-14 minutes	24
15-29 minutes	16
30 minutes - less than 1 hour	5
1 hour or more	10
Whether would like to give up smoking	
Yes	41
No	54
Don't know	5
Base	75

* Data available for subject interviews only

Table 3.21 Alcohol consumption of cigarette smokers compared with non–smokers

Residents with neurotic disorders*

	Mean units of alcohol per week	Median units of alcohol per week	*Base*
Smokers	9.2	2.7	*75*
Non-Smokers	[16.4]	[0.1]	*26*
All	11.0	1.5	*101*

* Data available for subject interviews only

Appendix A Measuring psychiatric morbidity

A.1 Calculation of CIS-R symptom scores

Fatigue

Scores relate to fatigue or feeling tired or lacking in energy in the past week.

Score one for each of:
- Symptom present on four days or more
- Symptom present for more than three hours in total on any day
- Subject had to push him/herself to get things done on at least one occasion
- Symptom present when subject doing things he/she enjoys or used to enjoy at least once

Sleep problems

Scores relate to problems with getting to sleep, or otherwise, with sleeping more than is usual for the subject in the past week.

Score one for each of:
- Had problems with sleep for four nights or more
- Spent at least 1 hour trying to get to sleep on the night with least sleep
- Spent at least 1 hour trying to get to sleep on the night with least sleep
- Spent 3 hours or more truing to get to sleep on four nights or more
- Slept for at least 1 hour longer than usual for subject on any night
- Slept for at least 1 hour longer than usual for subject on any night
- Slept for more than 3 hours longer than usual for subject on four nights or more

Irritability

Scores relate to feelings of irritability, being short-tempered or angry in the past week.

Score one for each of:
- Symptom present for four days or more
- Symptom present for more than 1 hour on any day
- Wanted to shout at someone in past week (even if subject had not actually shouted)
- Had arguments, rows or quarrels or lost temper with someone and felt it was unjustified on at least one occasion

Worry

Scores relate to subject's experience of worry in the past week, other than worry about physical Health.

Score one for each of:
- Symptom present on 4 or more days
- Has been worrying too much in view of circumstances
- Symptom has been very unpleasant
- Symptom lasted over three hours in total on any day

Depression

Applies to subjects who felt sad, miserable or depressed or unable to enjoy or take an interest in things as much as usual, in the past week. Scores relate to the subject's experience in the past week.

Score one for each of:
- Unable to enjoy or take an interest in things as much as usual
- Symptom present on four days or more
- Symptom lasted for more than 3 hours in total on any day
- When sad, miserable or depressed subject did not become happier when something nice happened, or when in company

Depressive ideas

Applies to subjects who had a score of 1 for depression. Scores relate to experience in the past week.

Score one for each of:
- Felt guilty or blamed him/herself when things went wrong when it had not been his/her fault
- Felt not as good as other people
- Felt hopeless
- Felt that life isn't worth living
- Thought of killing him/herself

Anxiety

Scores relate to feeling generally anxious, nervous or tense in the past week. These feelings were not the result of a phobia.

Score one for each of:
- Symptom present on four or more days
- Symptom had been very unpleasant
- When anxious, nervous or tense, had one or more of following symptoms:
   heart racing or pounding
   hands sweating or shaking
   feeling dizzy
   difficulty getting breath
   butterflies in stomach
   dry mouth
   nausea or feeling as though he/she wanted to vomit

- Symptom present for more than three hours in total on any one day

Obsessions

Scores relate to the subject's experience of having repetitive unpleasant thoughts or ideas in the past week.
Score one for each of:
- Symptom present on four or more days
- Tried to stop thinking any of these thoughts
- Became upset or annoyed when had these thoughts
- Longest episode of the symptom was $1/4$ hour or longer

Concentration and forgetfulness

Scores relate to the subject's experience of concentration problems and forgetfulness in the past week.
Score one for each of:
- Symptoms present for four days or more
- Could not always concentrate on a TV programme, read a newspaper article or talk to someone without mind wandering
- Problems with concentration stopped subject from getting on with things he/she used to do or would have liked to do
- Forgot something important

Somatic symptoms

Scores relate to the subject's experience in the past week of any ache, pain or discomfort which was brought on or made worse by feeling low, anxious or stressed.
Score one for each of:
- Symptom present for four days or more
- Symptom lasted more than 3 hours on any day
- Symptom had been very unpleasant
- Symptom bothered subject when doing something interesting

Compulsions

Scores relate to the subject's experience of doing things over again when subject had already done them in the past week.
Score one for each of:
- Symptom present on four days or more
- Subject tried to stop repeating behaviour
- Symptom made subject upset or annoyed with him/herself
- Repeated behaviour three or more times when it had already been done

Phobias

Scores relate to subject's experience of phobias or avoidance in the past week
Score one for each of:
- Felt nervous/anxious about a situation or thing four or more times
- On occasions when felt anxious, nervous or tense, had one or more of following symptoms:
  heart racing or pounding
  hands sweating or shaking
  feeling dizzy
  difficulty getting breath
  butterflies in stomach
  dry mouth
  nausea or feeling as though he/she wanted to vomit
- Avoided situation or thing at least once because it would have made subject anxious, nervous or tense

Worry about physical health

Scores relate to experience of the symptom in the past week.
Score one for each of:
- Symptom present on four days or more
- Subject felt he/she had been worrying too much in view of actual health
- Symptom had been very unpleasant
- Subject could not be distracted by doing something else

Panic

Applies to subjects who felt anxious, nervous or tense in the past week and the scores relate to the resultant feelings of panic, or of collapsing and losing control in the past week.
Score one for each of:
- Symptom experienced once
- Symptom experienced more than once
- Symptom had been very unpleasant or unbearable
- An episode lasted longer than 10 minutes

A.2 Algorithms to produce ICD-10 psychiatric disorders

The mental disorders reported in Chapter 6 were produced from the CIS-R schedule which is described in Chapter 2 and reproduced in Appendix C. The production of the 6 categories of disorder shown in these tables occurred in 3 stages: first, the informants' responses to the CIS-R were used to produce specific ICD-10 diagnoses of neurosis.

This was done by applying the algorithms described below. Second, these specific neurotic disorders plus psychosis were arranged hierarchically and the 'highest' disorder assumed precedence. The actual precedence rules are described below. Finally, the range of ICD-10 diagnoses were grouped together to produce categories used in the calculation of prevalence. ·

It should be noted that as a result of the hierarchical coding described above, the diagnoses of the 6 neurotic disorders and the category of functional psychosis are exclusive: an individual included in the prevalence rates for one neurotic or psychotic disorder is not included in calculation of the rate for any other neurotic or psychotic disorder.

Algorithms for production of ICD-10 diagnoses of neurosis from the CIS-R ('scores' refer to CIS-R scores)

F32.00 Mild depressive episode without somatic symptoms

1. Symptom duration ≥ 2 weeks

2. *Two or more from:*

   - depressed mood
   - loss of interest
   - fatigue

3. *Two or three from:*

   - reduced concentration
   - reduced self-esteem
   - ideas of guilt
   - pessimism about future
   - suicidal ideas or acts
   - disturbed sleep
   - diminished appetite

4. Social impairment

5. *Fewer than four from:*

   - lack of normal pleasure /interest
   - loss of normal emotional reactivity
   - a.m. waking ≥ 2 hours early
   - loss of libido
   - diurnal variation in mood
   - diminished appetite
   - loss of ≥ 5% body weight
   - psychomotor agitation
   - psychomotor retardation

F32.01 Mild depressive episode with somatic symptoms

1. Symptom duration ≥ 2 weeks

2. *Two or more from:*

   - depressed mood
   - loss of interest
   - fatigue

3. *Two or three from:*

   - reduced concentration
   - reduced self-esteem
   - ideas of guilt
   - pessimism about future
   - suicidal ideas or acts
   - disturbed sleep
   - diminished appetite

4. Social impairment

5. *Four or more from:*

   - lack of normal pleasure /interest
   - loss of normal emotional reactivity
   - a.m. waking ≥ 2 hours early
   - loss of libido
   - diurnal variation in mood
   - diminished appetite
   - loss of 5% body weight
   - psychomotor agitation
   - psychomotor retardation

F32.10 Moderate depressive episode without somatic symptoms

1. Symptom duration ≥2 weeks

2. *Two or more from:*

   - depressed mood
   - loss of interest
   - fatigue

3. *Four or more from:*

   - reduced concentration
   - reduced self-esteem
   - ideas of guilt
   - pessimism about future
   - suicidal ideas or acts
   - disturbed sleep
   - diminished appetite

4. Social impairment

5. *Fewer than four* from:

- lack of normal pleasure/interest
- loss of normal emotional reactivity
- a.m. waking ≥ 2 hours early
- loss of libido
- diurnal variation in mood
- diminished appetite
- loss of ≥ 5% body weight
- psychomotor agitation
- psychomotor retardation

F32.11 Moderate depressive episode with somatic symptoms

1. Symptom duration ≥2 weeks

2. *Two or more* from:

- depressed mood
- loss of interest
- fatigue

3. *Four or more* from:

- reduced concentration
- reduced self-esteem
- ideas of guilt
- pessimism about future
- suicidal ideas or acts
- disturbed sleep
- diminished appetite

4. Social impairment

5. *Four or more* from:

- lack of normal pleasure /interest
- loss of normal emotional reactivity
- a.m. waking ≥2 hours early
- loss of libido
- diurnal variation in mood
- diminished appetite
- loss of ≥ 5% body weight
- psychomotor agitation
- psychomotor retardation

F32.2 Severe depressive episode

1. *All three* from:

- depressed mood
- loss of interest
- fatigue

2. *Four or more* from:

- reduced concentration
- reduced self-esteem
- ideas of guilt
- pessimism about future
- suicidal ideas or acts
- disturbed sleep
- diminished appetite

3. Social impairment

4. *Four or more* from:

- lack of normal pleasure /interest
- loss of normal emotional reactivity
- a.m. waking ≥ 2 hours early
- loss of libido
- diurnal variation in mood
- diminished appetite
- loss of ≥ 5% body weight
- psychomotor agitation
- psychomotor retardation

F40.00 Agoraphobia without panic disorder
1. Fear of open spaces and related aspects: crowds, distance from home, travelling alone
2. Social impairment
3. Avoidant behaviour must be prominent feature
4. Overall phobia score ≥ 2
5. No panic attacks

F40.01 Agoraphobia with panic disorder
1. Fear of open spaces and related aspects: crowds, distance from home, travelling alone
2. Social impairment
3. Avoidant behaviour must be prominent feature
4. Overall phobia score ≥ 2
5. Panic disorder (overall panic score ≥ 2)

F40.1 Social phobias
1. Fear of scrutiny by other people: eating or speaking in public etc.
2. Social impairment
3. Avoidant behaviour must be prominent feature
4. Overall phobia score ≥ 2

F40.2 Specific (isolated) phobias
1. Fear of specific situations or things, e.g. animals, insects, heights, blood, flying, etc.
2. Social impairment
3. Avoidant behaviour must be prominent feature
4. Overall phobia score ≥ 2

F41.0 Panic disorder

1. Criteria for phobic disorders not met
2. Recent panic attacks
3. Anxiety-free between attacks
4. Overall panic score ≥ 2

F41.1 Generalised Anxiety Disorder

1. Duration ≥ 6 months
2. Free-floating anxiety
3. Autonomic overactivity
4. Overall anxiety score ≥ 2

F41.2 Mixed anxiety and depressive disorder

1. (Sum of scores for each CIS-R section) ≥ 12
2. Criteria for other categories not met

F42 Obsessive-Compulsive Disorder

1. Duration ≥ 2 weeks
2. At least one act/thought resisted
3. Social impairment
4. Overall scores:

    obsession score=4, or

    compulsion score=4, or

    obsession+compulsion scores ≥ 6

Hierarchical organisation of psychiatric disorders

The following rules (see table below) were used to allocate individuals who received more than one diagnosis of neurosis to the appropriate category.

Grouping neurotic and psychotic disorders into broad categories

The final step was to group some of the diagnoses into broad diagnostic categories prior to analysis.

Depressive episode

F32.00 and F32.01 were grouped to produce mild depressive episode (i.e. with or without somatic symptoms). F32.10 and F32.11 were similarly grouped to produce moderate depressive episode. Mild depressive episode, moderate depressive episode and Severe depressive episode (F32.2) were then combined to produce the final category of depressive episode.

Phobias

The ICD-10 phobic diagnoses F40.00, F40.01, F40.1 and F40.2, were combined into one category of phobia.

This produced six categories of neurosis for analysis:

    Mixed anxiety and depressive disorder

    Generalised Anxiety Disorder

    Depressive episode

    All phobias

    Obsessive Compulsive Disorder

    Panic disorder

Disorder 1	Disorder 2	Priority
Depressive episode (any severity)	Phobia	Depressive episode (any severity)
Depressive episode (mild)	OCD	OCD
Depressive episode (moderate)	OCD	Depressive episode (moderate)
Depressive episode (severe)	OCD	Depressive episode (severe)
Depressive episode (mild)	Panic disorder	Panic disorder
Depressive episode (moderate)	Panic disorder	Depressive episode (moderate)
Depressive episode (any severity)	GAD	Depressive episode (any severity)
Phobia (any)	OCD	OCD
Agoraphobia	GAD	Agoraphobia
Social phobia	GAD	Social phobia
Specific phobia	GAD	GAD
Panic disorder	OCD	Panic disorder
OCD	GAD	OCD
Panic disorder	GAD	Panic disorder

GAD = Generalised Anxiety Disorder; OCD = Obsessive– Compulsive Disorder

A3 Non-neurotic disorders

All psychiatric disorders with the exception of neuroses were assessed from self-reports by patients or their staff. Sometimes residents did not use medical terms to describe their conditions: how their answers were interpreted into ICD-10 diagnostic categories is shown below:

Primary diagnosis (based on ICD-10)

F00 - F09 Organic Mental Disorders
Dementia
Alzheimer's Disease

F10 - F19 Mental and behavioural disorders due to psychoactive substance use
Alcohol/heavy drinker
Opium
Cannabis
Sedatives
Cocaine
Stimulants
Hallucinogens
Tobacco
Volatile solvents
Any mixture of above

F20 - F29 Schizophrenia, schizotypal and delusional disorders
Catatonic schizophrenia
Chronic schizophrenia
Hebephrenic schizophrenia
High schizophrenia
Mild schizophrenia
Paranoid schizophrenia
Schizophrenia
Simple schizophrenia

Auditory hallucinations
Hallucinations
Hearing voices
Mild psychosis
Psychosis
Psychotic tendencies
Schizo-affective disorder
Schizophrenic affective disorder
Voices

F30 - F39 Mood (affective) disorders (excluding depressive episode)
Mania
Hyperactive
Hypomania
Mania
Manic depressive disorder
Bipolar affective disorder
Manic depression
Manic depressive psychosis
Moods
Mood swings

F50 - F59 Behavioural syndromes associated with physiological disturbance and physical factors
Anorexia nervosa
Bulimia nervosa
Sleep disorders (non-organic), nightfrights
Sexual disorders (non-organic)
Other behavioural syndromes

F60 - F69 Disorders of adult personality and behaviour
Habit and impulse disorders
Gender identity problems
Other personality disorders

F70 - F79 Mental retardation
Mental handicap
Backward or slow

F80 - F89 Disorders of psychological development

F90 - F98 Behavioural and emotional disorders with onset usually occurring in childhood and adolescence

Unspecified mental disorder
Mental illness
Mentally disturbed
Neuropathy

Appendix B Comparison of the characteristics of respondents and proxy informants

Table 1 Type of disorder by type of interview

Type of disorder	Type of interview			
	Subject	Proxy	Both	All
	%	%	%	%
Schizophrenia, delusional or schizoaffective	77	90	89	81
Affective psychoses	9	10	8	9
Neurotic	14	-	3	10
Base	*704*	*269*	*53*	*1025*
% of men and women with each type of interview	69%	26%	5%	100%

Table 2 Type of interview by type of mental illness and type of institution

Type of interview	Residents with schizophrenia, delusional or schizoaffective disorders						Residents with affective psychoses			Residents with neurotic disorders
	Hospitals and nursing homes	Residential care homes	Group homes	Hostels	Ordinary housing/ recognised lodging	All	Hospitals clinics and nursing homes	Other accommodation	All	
	%	%	%	%	%	%	%	%	%	%
Subject	55	67	84	73	74	65	50	85	66	98
Proxy	40	27	15	15	16	29	48	8	29	-
Both	5	6	1	12	10	6	2	6	4	2
Base	*359*	*193*	*113*	*73*	*71*	*828*	*51*	*45*	*96*	*101*
Reasons for proxy interviews										
subject incapable-mental problem	78	56	[8]	[8]	[10]	66	[22]	[3]	78	[1]
subject absent	6	3	[3]	[7]	[-]	8	[0]	[1]	4	[1]
subject had hearing/speech problem	1	-	[-]	[-]	[3]	2	[-]	[-]	[-]	[-]
subject too ill	1	2	[1]	[-]	[-]	1	[2]	[-]	[-]	[-]
subject did not speack English	0	2	[-]	[-]	[-]	1	[-]	[-]	[-]	[-]
other	14	38	[7]	[5]	[6]	23	[2]	[2]	14	[1]
Base	*161*	*61*	*18*	*19*	*18*	*283*	*26*	*7*	*32*	*2*

Table 3 Personal characteristics of residents by type of interview and type of mental illness

	Residents with schizophrenia, delusional or schixoaffective disorders				Residents with affective psychoses			Residents with neurotic disorders
	Type of interview				Type of interview			
	Subject	Proxy	Both	All	Subject/both	Proxy	All	
	%	%	%	%	%	%	%	%
Sex								
Male	73	68	61	71	60	[15]	42	39
Female	27	32	39	29	40	[13]	42	39
Age								
16-24	5	6	-	5	11	[4]4	12	21
25-34	19	22	24	20	17	[13]	25	18
35-44	26	20	17	23	26	[1]	20	21
45-54	31	25	21	29	26	[7]	26	20
55-64	20	27	38	23	20	[3]	17	20
Marital status								
Married/conhabiting	3	3	6	3	5	[1]	4	12
Single	79	83	77	80	61	[21]	65	65
Widowed	2	1	5	2	2	[1]	2	1
Divorced	14	11	12	13	29	[3]	24	19
Separated	2	2	-	2	4	[2]	4	3
Type of institution								
Hospital, clinic or nursing home	36	60	39	43	39	[25]	53	20
Residential care home	24	21	25	23	28	[2]	22	32
Group homes	18	7	3	14	19	[2]	15	18
Hostels	10	4	15	9	5	[-]	4	23
Ordinary housing/recognised lodging	10	5	15	9	8	[-]	6	7
Base	*541*	*240*	*47*	*828*	*68*	*28*	*96*	*101*

Glossary of survey definitions and terms

Activities of Daily Living

The seven area of functioning covered by the survey were:

- **Personal care** such as dressing, bathing, washing, or using the toilet.

- **Using transport** to get out and about.

- **Medical care** such as taking medicines or pills, having injections or changes of dressing.

- **Household activities** such as preparing meals, shopping, laundry and housework.

- **Practical activities** such as gardening, decorating or doing household repairs.

- **Dealing with paperwork**, such as writing letters, sending cards or filling in forms.

- **Managing money** such as budgeting for food or paying bills.

Respondents were asked whether they had difficulty with each task. Apart from the responses, 'Yes' and 'No', there was also a 'Does Not Apply' category which was used when the activity was not in the daily repertoire of behaviours of the subject. Care was taken that if the activity was not carried out because of a physical or mental health problem, the subject was deemed to have difficulty in carrying out the task.

Adults

In this survey adults were defined as persons aged 16 or over and less than aged 65.

Alcohol consumption

The final classification of alcohol consumption required the amalgamation of detailed information on what alcohol was drunk and the frequency of intake converted into units. The several stages involved in this process were:

1. Establishing how often the subject had the following drinks:

   - **Shandy** (excluding bottles or cans)

- **Beer, lager, stout or cider**

- **Spirits or liqueurs** (eg. gin, whisky, rum, brandy, vodka, avocaat)

- **Wine** (including Babycham and champagne)

- **Any other alcoholic drink**

2. For any drink taken in the last year, how much was usually drunk on any one day.

3. Converting measures (pints, cans, singles, glasses) into units.

4. Taking account of the different evaluation of units of alcohol for women and men .

The final classification of weekly alcohol consumption rating was:

- **Abstainer**

- **Occasional** - Men (<1); Women (<1)

- **Light** - Men (1-10); Women (1-7)

- **Moderate** - Men (11-21); Women (8-14)

- **Fairly heavy** - Men (22-35); Women (15-25)

- **Heavy** - Men (36-50); Women (26-35)

- **Very heavy** - Men (51+); Women (36+)

Alcohol dependence

This was derived from responses to a self-completion questionnaire asked of all survey respondents. Individuals were classified as alcohol dependent if they had three or more positive responses to the following twelve statements.

Loss of control

1. Once I started drinking it was difficult for me to stop before I became completely drunk

2. I sometimes kept on drinking after I had promised myself not to.

3. I deliberately tried to cut down or stop drinking, but I was unable to do so.

4. Sometimes I have needed a drink so badly that I could not think of anything else.

Symptomatic behaviour

5. I have skipped a number of regular meals while drinking

6. I have often had an alcoholic drink the first thing when I got up in the morning.

7. I have had a strong drink in the morning to get over the previous night's drinking

8. I have woken up the next day not being able to remember some of the things I had done while drinking.

9. My hand shook a lot in the morning after drinking.

10. I need more alcohol than I used to get the same effect as before.

11. Sometimes I have woken up during the night or early morning sweating all over because of drinking.

Binge Drinking

12. I have stayed drunk for several days at a time.

Antipsychotic drugs
These are also known as 'neuroleptics'. In the short term they are used to quieten disturbed patients whatever the underlying psychopathology.
See Depot Injections

Cigarette smoking
Questions on cigarette smoking were taken from the General Household Survey. For those who did smoke the average number of cigarettes smoked per day was calculated from answers to questions on the number of cigarettes usually smoked on weekdays and on weekends. The final classification did not take account of the tar level of cigarettes, only the quantity smoked:

• **Light smoker** - less than 10 a day

• **Moderate smoker** - more than 10 but less than 20 a day

• **Heavy smoker** - at least 20 a day

• **Ex-regular smoker**

• **Never a regular smoker**

Depot injections
When antipsychotic medication is given by injections on a monthly basis, these are sometimes termed depot injections.

Drug dependence
This was derived from responses to a self-completion questionnaire asked of all survey respondents. An individual was classified as drug dependent if they had a positive response to any of the following five questions in relation to the 10 drugs listed in the box below. A prerequisite was that the drug(s) must have been taken either without a prescription, more than was prescribed for the subject, or to get high.

> 1. Sleeping Pills, Barbiturates, Sedatives, Downers, Seconal
>
> 2. Tranquillisers, Valium, Librium
>
> 3. Cannabis, Marijuana, Hash, Dope, Grass, Ganja, Kif
>
> 4. Amphetamines, Speed, Uppers, Stimulants, Qat
>
> 5. Cocaine, Coke, Crack
>
> 6. Heroin, Smack
>
> 7. Opiates other than heroin: Demerol, Morphine, Methadone, Darvon,Opium, DF118
>
> 8. Psychedelics, Hallucinogens: LSD, Mescaline, Acid, Peyote, Psylocybin (Magic) mushrooms
>
> 9. Ecstasy
>
> 10. Solvents, inhalants, glue, amyl nitrate

1. Have you ever used any one of these drugs every day for two weeks or more in the past twelve months?

2. In the past twelve months have you used any one of these drugs to the extent that you felt like you needed it or were dependent on it?

3. In the past twelve months, have you tried to cut down on any drugs but found you could not do it?

4. In the past twelve months did you find that you needed larger amounts of these drugs to get an

effect, or that you could no longer get high on the amount you used to use?

5. In the past twelve months have you had withdrawal symptoms such as feeling sick because you stopped or cut down on any of these drugs?

Drug use

Information was initially collected on the use of particular groups of drugs. This was subsumed under more general headings for the purpose of analysis.

- **Cannabis**

- **Stimulants** (cocaine and speed)

- **Hallucinogens** (acid and Ecstasy)

- **Hypnotics** (barbiturates, sedatives, tranquillisers, valium, librium, etc)

- **Other** - heroin, opium, solvents

A subject was classified as having used drugs in the past year if he/she had taken any of these drugs in the past 12 months either without a prescription, more than was prescribed, or to get high, and had taken the drug more than five times in his/her life.

Economic activity

The questions used to measure economic activity were taken from those regularly asked in the General Household Survey. All adults are place into one of eight categories:

- **Working** - having done paid work in the seven days ending the Sunday before the interview, either as an employee or self-employed, including those were not actually at work but had a job they were away from.

- **Looking for work**

- **Intending to look for work** but prevented by temporary, ill-health, sickness or injury

- **Going to school or college full-time** - only used for persons aged 16-49.

- **Permanently unable to work** due to long-term sickness or disability - for women, only used if aged 16-59

- **Retired** - used only if stopped work at the aged of 50 or over

- **Looking after the home or family**

- **Other** - doing something else

Educational level

Educational level was based on the highest educational qualification obtained and was grouped as follows:

Degree (or degree level qualification)

Teaching, HND, Nursing
      Teaching qualification
      HNC/HND, BEC/TEC Higher, BTEC
Higher
      City and Guilds Full Technological
      Certificate
      Nursing qualifications:
      (SRN,SCM,RGN,RM,RHV,
      Midwife)

A level
      GCE A-levels/SCE higher
      ONC/OND/BEC/TEC/not higher
      City and Guilds Advanced/Final level
O level
      GCE O-level (grades A-C if after 1975)
      GCSE (grades A-C)
      CSE (grade 1)
      SCE Ordinary (bands A-C)
      Standard grade (levels 1-3)
      SLC Lower SUPE Lower or Ordinary
      School certificate or Matric
      City and Guilds Craft/Ordinary level

GCSE/CSE
      GCE O-level (grades D-E if after 1975)
      GCSE (grades D-G)
      CSE (grades 2-5)
      SCE Ordinary (bands D-E)
      Standard grade (levels 4-5)
      Clerical or commercial qualifications
      Apprenticeship
      Other qualifications

No qualifications
      CSE ungraded
      No qualifications

Employment status

Four types of employment status were identified: working full time, working part time, unemployed and economically inactive.

Working adults

The two categories of working adults include persons who did any work for pay or profit in the week ending the last Sunday prior to interview, even if it was for as little as one hour, including Saturday jobs and casual work (e.g. babysitting, running a mail order club).

Self-employed persons were considered to be working if they worked in their own business, professional practice, or farm for the purpose of making a profit, or even if the enterprise was failing to make a profit or just being set up.

The unpaid 'family worker' (e.g., a wife doing her husband's accounts or helping with the farm or business) was included as working if the work contributed directly to a business, farm or family practice owned or operated by a related member of the same household. (Although the individual concerned may have received no pay or profit, her contribution to the business profit counted as paid work.) This only applied when the business was owned or operated by a member of the same household.

Anyone on a Government scheme which was employer based was also 'working last week'.

Informants' definitions dictated whether they felt they were working full time or part time.

Unemployed adults
This category included those who were waiting to take up a job that had already been obtained, those who were looking for work, and people who intended to look for work but were prevented by temporary ill-health, sickness or injury. 'Temporary' was defined by the informant.

Economically inactive
This category comprised five main categories of people:

'Going to school or college' only applied to people who were under 50 years of age. The category included people following full-time educational courses at school or at further education establishments (colleges, university, etc). It included all school children (16 years and over).

During vacations, students were treated as 'going to school or college' even where their return to college was dependent on passing a set of exams. If however, they were having a break from full-time education, i.e. they were taking a year out, they were not counted as being in full-time education.

'Permanently unable to work because of long-term sickness or disability' only applied to those under state retirement age, ie to men aged 16 to 64 and to women aged 16 to 59. 'Permanently' and 'long-term' were defined by the informant.

'Retired' only applied to those who retired from their full-time occupation at age 50 or over and were not seeking further employment of any kind.

'Looking after the home or family' covered anyone who was mainly involved in domestic duties, provided this person had not already been coded in an earlier category.

'Doing something else' included anyone for whom the earlier categories were inappropriate.

Ethnicity
Household members were classified into nine groups by the person answering Schedule A.

White	White
Black - Caribbean Black - African Black - Other	West Indian/African
Indian Pakistani Bangladeshi Chinese	Asian/Oriental
None of these	Other

For analysis purpose these nine groups were subsumed under 4 headings: White, West Indian/African, Asian/Oriental and Other.

Marital status
Informants were categorised according to their own perception of marital status. Married and cohabiting took priority over other categories. Cohabiting included anyone living together with their partner as a couple.

Perceived social support
The level of social support which informants reported was based on responses to the following 7 statements. Respondents could say that each statement was not true, partly true or certainly true.

There are people I know – amongst my family or friends – who...

1. do things to make me happy
2. make me feel loved
3. can be relied on no matter what happens
4. would see that I am taken care of if I needed to be

5. accept me just as I am
6. make me feel an important part of their lives
7. give me support and encouragement

Each response of not true scored 1, partly true scored 2 and certainly true scored 3; individuals therefore had a total score of between 7 and 21.

Social support was classified as:

> severe lack (scores 7 to 17)
> moderate lack (scores 18 to 20)
> no lack (score 21)

Physical complaints

Informants were asked 'Do you have any long-standing illness, disability or infirmity? By long-standing I mean anything that has troubled you over a period of time or that is likely to affect you over a period of time?'

Those that answered yes to this question were then asked 'What is the matter with you?'; interviewers were asked to try and obtain a medical diagnosis, or to establish the main symptoms. From these responses, illnesses were coded to the site or system of the body that was affected, using a classification system that roughly corresponded to the chapter headings of the International Classification of Diseases (ICD–10). Some of the illnesses identified were mental illnesses and these were excluded from the classification of physical illness. Physical illness did, however, include physical disabilities and sensory complaints such as eyesight and hearing problems.

Primary support group

The size of the individual's primary support group was calculated as a measure of the extent of their social networks. In the survey, data were collected about the size of three groups of people:

The **number of adults who lived with the respondent** that they felt close to, including staff living on the premises

The **number of relatives who did not live with the respondent** that they felt close to

The **number of friends or acquaintances who did not live with the respondent** that would be described as close or good friends

The total number of close friends and relatives were regarded as the individual's primary support group. For the purposes of analysis, the total number in the primary support group was categorised into: 3 or fewer, 4-8, and 9 or more.

Psychiatric morbidity

The expression psychiatric morbidity refers to the degree or extent of the prevalence of mental health problems within a defined area.

Printed in the United Kingdom for HMSO
Dd. 0302177 C12 5/96 48186